180

D0015536

# Alone
# Time

# Alone
# Time

Four Seasons,
Four Cities,
and the
Pleasures of Solitude

Stephanie Rosenbloom

Viking

VIKING
An imprint of Penguin Random House LLC
375 Hudson Street
New York, New York 10014
penguin.com

LIBRARY OF CONGRESS CATALOGING-IN-PUBLICATION DATA
Names: Rosenbloom, Stephanie, author.
Title: Alone time : four seasons, four cities, and the pleasures of solitude / Stephanie Rosenbloom.
Description: New York, New York : Viking, [2018] |
Identifiers: LCCN 2018011925 (print) | LCCN 2018015035 (ebook) | ISBN 9780399562310 (ebook) | ISBN 9780399562303 (hardcover)
Subjects: LCSH: Travelers—Psychology. | Solitude. | Rosenbloom, Stephanie—Travel. | BISAC: BODY, MIND & SPIRIT / Inspiration & Personal Growth. | TRAVEL / Essays & Travelogues. | BIOGRAPHY & AUTOBIOGRAPHY / Personal Memoirs.
Classification: LCC G155.A1 (ebook) | LCC G155.A1 R625 2018 (print) | DDC 910.401/9—dc23
LC record available at https://lccn.loc.gov/2018011925

Printed in the United States of America
10  9  8  7  6  5  4  3  2  1

Set in Albertina MT Pro
Designed by Nancy Resnick

For Daniel
&
my parents

# Contents

# Alone
# Time

# Introduction: Witches and Shamans

$P$*aris; June.* The taxi rolled to a stop in front of 22 rue de la Parcheminerie. It was Saturday morning, before the café chairs were put out, before visitors began arriving at the old church, before check-in time at the little hotel with its window boxes of red geraniums.

Cigarette butts and red petals were scattered across the sidewalk.

I was alone with a suitcase and a reservation. And days to live however I chose.

———

> *The average adult spends about one-third of his or her waking time alone.*
>
> —Mihaly Csikszentmihalyi, *Flow*

How are you spending yours? Scrolling Facebook? Texting? Tweeting? Online shopping? The to-do list is endless.

But time isn't.

Alone time is an invitation, a chance to do the things you've longed to do. You can read, code, paint, meditate, practice a language, or go for a stroll.

Alone, you can pick through sidewalk crates of used books without worrying you're hijacking your companion's afternoon or being judged for your lousy idea of a good time. You need not carry on polite conversation. You can go to a park. You can go to Paris.

You'd hardly be alone. From North America to South Korea more people are now living by themselves than ever before. Single-person households are projected to be the fastest-growing household profile globally from today to 2030. More people are dining solo. More are traveling alone—a lot more. From vacation rental companies to luxury tour operators, industry groups have been reporting double-digit upticks in solo travel. Airbnb is seeing more solo travelers than ever. Intrepid Travel reports that half of its guests—some seventy-five thousand people a year—are now traveling by themselves, leading the company to create its very first solos only tours. And the boom isn't being driven just by people who are single: The "married-with-kids" solo traveler market is growing as well. Nearly 10 percent of American travelers with partners and children are taking solo vacations during the year, according to one of the world's largest travel marketing organizations, MMGY Global. In other words, traveling alone isn't just for twentysomethings and retirees, but for anyone who wants it, at any age, in any situation: partners, parents, and singles looking for romance—or not.

Few of us want to be recluses. The rise of coworking and co-living spaces around the world is but the latest evidence of that. Yet having a little time to ourselves, be it five days in Europe or five minutes in our backyard, can be downright enviable.

Some 85 percent of adults—both men and women, across all age groups—told the Pew Research Center that it's important for them to be completely alone sometimes. A survey by Euromonitor International found that people want more time not only with their families, but also by themselves. And yet many of us, even those who cherish alone time, are often reluctant to do certain things on our own—which may lead us to miss out on entertaining, enriching, even life-changing experiences and new relationships.

A series of studies published in the *Journal of Consumer Research* found that men and women were likely to avoid enjoyable public activities like going to a movie or restaurant if they had no one to accompany them. Any potential pleasure and inspiration that might come from seeing a great film or an art show was outweighed by their belief that going alone wouldn't be as much fun, not to mention their concerns about how they might be perceived by others.

Indeed, for many of us, solitude is something to be avoided, something associated with problems like loneliness and depression. Freud observed that "the first situation phobias of children are darkness and solitude." In many preliterate cultures, solitude was thought to be practically intolerable, as the psychologist Mihaly Csikszentmihalyi wrote in *Flow*, his book about the science of happiness: "Only witches and shamans feel comfortable spending time by themselves."

Perhaps it's not surprising that a series of studies published in the journal *Science* in 2014 found that many participants preferred to administer an electric shock to themselves rather than be left alone with their own thoughts for fifteen minutes. Man, as scientists and philosophers from Aristotle on have noted, is a social animal. And with good reason. Positive relationships are crucial to our survival; to humanity's collective knowledge, progress, and joy. One of the longest studies of adult life in history, the Harvard Study of Adult Development, has tracked hundreds of men for nearly eighty years, and the takeaway again and again has been that good relationships—with family, friends, colleagues, and people in our communities—make for happy, healthy lives.

Socially isolated people, on the other hand, are at an increased risk for disease and cognitive decline. As Robert Waldinger, the director of the Harvard study, has not so subtly put it: "Loneliness kills." Christian hermits broke up their solitary periods with communal work and worship. Thoreau had three chairs in his house in the woods, "one for solitude, two for friendship, three for society." Even the Lone Ranger had Tonto. Solitude and its perils is an ancient and instructive story.

But it's not the whole story. The company of others, while fundamental, is not the only way of finding fulfillment in our lives.

For centuries people have been retreating into solitude—for spirituality, creativity, reflection, renewal, and meaning. Buddhists and Christians entered monasteries. Native Americans went up mountains and into valleys. Audrey Hepburn took to her apartment. "I have to be alone very often," she told *Life* magazine in 1953. "I'd be quite happy if I spent from Saturday night until Monday morning alone in my apartment. That's how I refuel."

Others went great distances. Miles were sailed, flown, and driven by solo adventurers like Captain Joshua Slocum and Anne-France Dautheville, one of the first women to ride a motorcycle alone around the world. "From now on, my life would be mine, my way," she said of riding solo 12,500 miles in 1973.

Scholars have been insisting for decades that the positive aspects of solitude deserve a closer look, from the pediatrician and psychoanalyst Donald Winnicott in the 1950s to the British psychiatrist Anthony Storr in the 1980s, to psychologists leading studies today. A little solitude, their research suggests, can be good for us.

For one thing, time spent away from the influence of others allows us to explore and define who we are. In private, we can think deeply and independently, as the legal scholar and privacy expert Alan Westin explained. There's room for problem solving, experimentation, and imagination. The mind can crackle with intense focus or go beachcombing, plucking up an idea like a shell, examining and pocketing it, or letting it go to pick up another.

Thinkers, artists, and innovators from Tchaikovsky to Barack Obama, from Delacroix and Marcel Marceau to Chrissie Hynde and Alice Walker, have expressed the need for solitude. It's what Rodin has in common with Amy Schumer; what Michelangelo shares with Grace Jones. Philosophers and scientists spent much of their lives in solitude, including Descartes, Nietzsche, and Barbara McClintock, the Nobel Prize–winning geneticist who resisted having a telephone until she was eighty-four. Countless writers, including Shakespeare, Dickinson, Wharton, Hugo, and Huxley, mined solitude as a theme. Symphonies and songs, poems and plays, and paintings and photos have been created *in* solitude.

For the creative person, "his most significant moments are those in which he attains some new insight, or makes some new discovery; and these moments are chiefly, if not invariably, those in which he is alone," Storr wrote in his seminal book, *Solitude: A Return to the Self.* While other people can be one of our greatest sources of happiness, they can at times nonetheless be a distraction. Their presence may also inhibit the creative process, "since creation is embarrassing," as the writer Isaac Asimov said. "For every new good idea you have, there are a hundred, ten thousand foolish ones, which you naturally do not care to display." Monet slashed his paintings before the opening of an exhibition in Paris, declaring the canvasses unworthy to pass on to posterity. Robert Rauschenberg flung his early works into the Arno.

Yet just as alone time can be important for creation (and possible subsequent destruction), it can also be necessary for restoration. Some of the latest research has found that even fifteen minutes spent by ourselves, without electronic devices or social interaction, can decrease the intensity of our feelings (be they good or bad), leaving us more easygoing, less angry, and less worried. Studies led by Thuy-vy Nguyen, published in the *Personality and Social Psychology Bulletin,* suggest that we can use solitude or alone time as a tool, a way to regulate our emotional states, "becoming quiet after excitement, calm after an angry episode, or centered and peaceful when desired."

Alone, we can power down. We're "off stage," as the sociologist Erving Goffman put it, where we can doff the mask we wear in public and be ourselves. We can be reflective. We have the opportunity for self-evaluation, a chance to consider our actions and take what Westin called a "moral inventory."

We can also take inventory of all the information that has accumulated throughout the day. We can organize our "thoughts, reflect on past actions and future plans, and prepare for future encounters," as the psychologist Jerry M. Burger wrote in the *Journal of Research in Personality*. Even Bill Clinton, exemplar of extraversion, acknowledged that as president he scheduled "a couple of hours a day alone to think, reflect, plan, or do nothing." "Often," he said, "I slept less just to get the alone time."

This notion of reflection harks back to an ancient Greek principle known as *epimelesthai sautou*. The philosopher Michel Foucault translated it as "to take care of yourself," and though it was once "one of the main rules for social and personal conduct and for the art of life," Foucault observed that there is a tendency, particularly in modern Western society, to view caring for oneself as almost immoral.

And yet alone time has the potential to leave us more open and compassionate toward others. John D. Barbour, a professor of religion at St. Olaf College in Northfield, Minnesota, has written that while solitude involves the self, it's not necessarily narcissistic. He's suggested that the solitude sought by biblical prophets helped shape their perspective and may have made them more sensitive to the suffering of people who were less powerful or outsiders. "Solitude at its best," he wrote, is not about "escaping the world, but toward a different kind of participation in it."

Unfortunately, there's a tendency in our own age of scant nuance to conceive of solitude and society as either-or propositions: You're either alone on your couch or you're organizing dinner parties. That's an unhelpful (and often wrong) distinction. The psychologist Abraham H. Maslow found that self-actualizing people—those who have attained the highest tier of his hierarchy of human needs—are capable of being more than one thing at one time, even if those things are contradictory. They can be simultaneously individual and social; selfish and unselfish. Burger wrote that people with a high preference for solitude don't necessarily dislike social interaction, and aren't necessarily introverted. They probably spend most of their time around others, and enjoy it; he said it's simply that, relative to others, they more often chose to be by themselves because they appreciate the reflection, creativity, and renewal that solitude can offer.

For years, the conventional wisdom was that if you spent a good deal of time alone, something was likely wrong with you. And, certainly, as psychologists have observed, many people do withdraw because they're socially anxious or depressed. Yet many others choose to spend time alone because they find it pleasurable. Maslow, for example, said that mature, self-actualizing people are particularly drawn to privacy, detachment, and meditativeness.

Indeed, one of the keys to enjoying alone time appears to be whether or not it's voluntary. Additional factors, like what people think about when they're alone, their age, and whether the time alone is temporary, may also play a role, but choice—taking some time to yourself because it's what you desire, and not because you've been abandoned by your social network or have no other option—seems to be crucial. It can be the difference between a positive experience of solitude and excessive loneliness.

How much time alone feels right, however, is a matter of taste and circumstance. For some, time alone is a rare privilege; something desired but hard to get between long work hours and a full house. Others may feel they spend too much time by themselves. Finding a balance that feels good is personal, and not necessarily easy.

In the months before he became engaged, Charles Darwin, who famously wrote about man's dislike of solitude and yet also prized his own solitary hours, created two columns in his journal headed "Marry" and "Not Marry." Under reasons to "Not Marry" he included "freedom to go where one liked"; "Loss of time"; and "cannot read in the Evenings." He continued on the following page: "I never should know French,—or see the Continent—or go to America, or go up in a Balloon, or take solitary trip in Wales."

But marriage, with its promise of companionship and children, prevailed. In a letter to his future wife, Emma, before their wedding day, Darwin told her that up to that point, he had rested his "notions of happiness on quietness & a good deal of solitude." However, he believed that with Emma, he might find happiness beyond "accumulating facts in silence & solitude." And for forty-three years, it seems he did.

At Down House, the Darwin home in rural Kent county outside London, he lazed on the grass with his children under lime trees, listened to family letters read aloud in the drawing room, and played backgammon with Emma. Still, he carved out alone time, retreating to his study for up to six hours a day. Outdoors, between what his granddaughter Gwen Raverat described as "two great lonely meadows," he built "the Sand-walk," a quarter-mile path around a wood that he walked almost daily, even circling it multiple times, while trying to solve a problem. It was in his study and on this "thinking path," as Darwin called it, amid old gnarled trees, bumblebees, and birds' nests, that he conducted experiments and wrote *On the Origin of Species*.

While Charles Darwin was in England strolling beneath tree boughs, another Charles—Baudelaire—was in Paris, writing about solitary journeys of a different sort.

Baudelaire's subject was Constantin Guys, the illustrator and journalist whose great pleasure was to wander the city's sidewalks. His "thinking path," unlike Darwin's, was paved and public, though no less a source of inspiration. It was Baudelaire's description of Guys's walks that established the archetype and fantasy of the *flâneur*: the solitary stroller, following his curiosity with no particular destination in mind, nowhere to be but in the here and now.

More than 150 years later, I went in search of that fantasy.

Months before I arrived at the little hotel with its red geraniums, I was in Paris on an assignment for the Travel section of the *New York Times*. I had five days and a headline: "Solo in Paris." The story was up to me.

To find it, I went walking. Each morning I left my hotel in the 9th arrondissement, just east of the apartment where Proust wrote much of *Remembrance of Things Past*, and didn't return until I had gone some twenty miles in whichever direction whim and croissants (and olive fougasse and pistachio financiers) took me.

It was April, and like any tourist I saw monuments and statues, naked nymphs, and gods among the roses. But alone, with no one at my side, I was also able to see *le merveilleux quotidien*, "the marvelous in everyday life": a golden retriever gazing at a café chalkboard in Montmartre, as if reading the daily specials; boxes of *pâtes de fruits* arranged in grids like Gerhard Richter's color charts. The city had my full attention; I was attuned to the faint whir of bicycle wheels and the scent of peaches at the street market.

Although I was traveling without friends or family, each day brought passing companions: bakers, maître d's, museum greeters, shopkeepers, fellow travelers. The hours were unhurried and entirely mine, like the "limitless solitude" the poet Rilke described in a letter to a friend; "this taking each day like a life-time, this being-with-everything."

Only, it wasn't a lifetime—it was five days. On the last morning, I slipped through a gate on rue de Rivoli into the Tuileries.

Sprinklers flung water into the air. A man with a wheelbarrow bent over a bed of long-stemmed tulips. John Russell, the British art critic, once wrote that the rue de Rivoli seemed to say to mankind, "This is what life can be . . . and now it's up to you to live it." That's what those days in Paris said to me. I wondered when, or if, I'd see the tulips again.

On assignment, I would play detective; partake of everything, get up early, record the details, do the things that felt strange and uncomfortable. But the assignment was over. Months passed and back in New York, the days grew shorter. Yet my head was still in Paris. It wasn't a matter of missing cream confections flirting in the windows of boulangeries. I missed who I *was* in Paris—the other me, Stéphanie with the accent on the "e": curious, improvisational, open to serendipity.

Finally, I took a long weekend to think about why I couldn't let go of that particular assignment, why alone in Paris time seemed to be on my side; why my senses pricked up; why I was able to delight in the smallest of things and yet failed to see and feel with such intensity at home. Friends loaned me their empty house near a bay on Long Island where on an autumn afternoon I stepped off a bus with a week's worth of reading and Chinese takeout. Without car or television, I spent days orbiting between a bench on the front porch and an oversize pink wing chair at the head of the dining room table, like the one at the Mad Hatter's tea party in the 1951 Disney film, eating vegetable lo mein and reading about different experiences of solitude. I plumbed newspaper archives and Gutenberg.org. I ordered used and out-of-print books. I wanted to know what scientists, writers, artists, musicians, and scholars thought about alone time, how they used it, why it mattered. Sometimes I walked a dead-end street to the bay. Other times I would lie on the wood floor in a patch of sun, staring at the ceiling, trying to deconstruct those solitary hours in Paris. There was something there; some way of living that I'd failed to fully grasp, let alone carry with me to my own city.

Yet the best way to understand the enchanted solitude I experienced in Paris wasn't to lie around thinking about it. It was to go back. Alone, of course.

If the *Times* assignment had been my introduction to the city, I would have dismissed my time there as just another spell cast on a sentimental American. But I'd been in Paris before. At the house by the bay I'd come to suspect it was the way in which I used alone time on the job, not just the beauty and splendor of the city, that made the days rich and meaningful. If I could figure out what I'd done differently on that trip, and why it felt so right so many months later, perhaps I could adopt similar practices—and evoke similar feelings—in my own backyard.

Back in New York I went online and booked a room—a photo of a little hotel with window boxes of red geraniums caught my eye—and planned my return to Paris.

Being in an unfamiliar place can lead to personal change, renewal, and discoveries. Anthony Storr said it's why many people find it easier to give up smoking when on vacation: It disrupts routine and day-to-day environmental cues that may be limiting or flat-out unhealthy. Indeed, my aim wasn't to master Paris. It was to master myself: to learn how a little alone time can change your life—in any city.

This book is the story of what I learned in Paris and in other places where I decided to spend time alone. I chose to explore cities, not the countryside, because I live in one; because in cities we can enjoy both privacy and society; because as Baudelaire wrote, "for the perfect *flâneur*, for the passionate spectator, it is an immense joy to set up house in the heart of the multitude."

At the house on the bay I winnowed the world to four cities—Paris, Istanbul, Florence, New York—one for each week of vacation I had in a year. (I would later revisit certain cities, and those moments appear in these pages as well.) I included New York because it's home; because I wanted to figure out how to recapture the awe of the outsider in a place so familiar to me that it had become invisible.

The other destinations beckoned for different reasons. I was taken with the architecture of Istanbul. I liked the thought of strolling Florence when the trees turn as yellow as the farmhouses on the hillsides. Yet all of the cities share certain qualities that spoke to me as a solo traveler. All have waterfronts, and none require a car. The idea of the *flâneur* may have originated in Paris, yet it was in Florence that Henry James declared himself a "charmed *flâneur*" in *Italian Hours*. It's alone on the back streets of Istanbul that Orhan Pamuk's characters seek solace and intrigue. It's on the sidewalks of New York that Walt Whitman sings of America. A number of cities, like Tokyo and Seoul, seemed impossible to omit, but there was the practical matter of my job, and with only a week at most to spare in each place, I ruled out locations that required too much flight time.

What follows are impressions of four journeys; a love letter to loners, to witches and shamans, to those who cherish their friends, spouses, and partners yet also want alone time to think, create, have an adventure, learn a skill, or solve a problem. I hope something in these pages helps you to find your "thinking path"; to discover what you want from your own solitary moments.

"When do you pause?" wrote Julia Child's husband, Paul, in the 1950s when the Childs were living in Paris. "When do you paint or pant? When write family, loll on moss, hear Mozart and watch the glitter of the sea?"

When you're alone.

## PART I

Spring

# Paris

# FOOD

# Café et Pluie ~ Coffee and Rain

*The Science of Savoring*

> *The word degustation means what it says: not "consumption of" but "tasting," "savoring" . . . You are in the country of the art of good food, and this degustation is very like what you do in an art gallery, unless your soul is lost.*
>
> —Eleanor Clark, *The Oysters of Locmariaquer*

Rue de la Parcheminerie runs between a river and a hill. Walk three minutes north and you'll be at the Seine; walk south and you'll find the Sorbonne. Part of the street is a graffitied pedestrian alley. The rest is a one-way passage beside a church with long-necked gargoyles and one of the oldest bells in Paris. In the middle of the street sits the little hotel with red geraniums, the Hôtel Parc Saint Séverin. There are twenty-seven rooms. One was mine.

Room 61 had all the desiderata for solitary pursuits: one bed, one slender wood writing desk, one bergère chair with a green velvety seat that sagged *just so*. In the closet: a small stack of books about France (bridges, the Louvre, Napoleon) and a few issues of *Madame Figaro* and *Vogue Paris*. There was scant floor space, though it didn't matter once the drapes were pulled back and the Roman shades tied up: Sunlight streamed through French doors and casement windows that opened to the rooftops of the Latin Quarter.

From the balcony you could see straight down rue Boutebrie to the Musée de Cluny and the market on boulevard Saint-Germain that sold sausage, foie gras, navettes from Marseilles, and biscuits from Provence. You could see over mansard roofs, weathercocks, and orange chimney pots to the dome of the Panthéon. To the east was a rose window of Notre-Dame; to the west, the tip of the Eiffel Tower.

In the morning, a man in boxers appeared on a nearby balcony to smoke and water his plants. In the afternoon, the Abbey Bookshop put wine crates of books on tables and stools in the street. In the evening, silverware clinked and voices floated up from tables that materialized outside the fondue joint next door.

One morning soon after I arrived, after the tables had been put away and the streets where students had walked arm in arm in the dark were empty again, I woke up to chirping and the faint shouting of children. I cracked the balcony doors and in came the distant swish of passing cars; the air cool and damp on my bare feet. Boys were kicking a ball around the churchyard. Bells chimed.

Time to begin. I pulled on jeans, a T-shirt, and my old leather jacket; tucked an umbrella in my bag; slid a finger through the tasseled keychain; and left room 61. At the end of the wallpapered hall I circled down six flights of corkscrew stairs to the lobby, past the pale blue sitting room with the morning pastry baskets, and handed the key to the woman at the desk, sprinkling in my wake the few French words I knew—*Bonjour, madame! Merci!*—as I breezed out the door onto rue de la Parcheminerie.

Parcheminerie takes its name from the parchment merchants who worked there in the Middle Ages, though one of dozens of volumes of the nineteenth-century series *Promenades dans toutes les rues de Paris* ("Walks in all the streets of Paris") says Parcheminerie was at one point known as rue des Écrivains, street of writers.

The philosopher and writer Denis Diderot had an apartment there in the 1700s. The photographer Eugène Atget began hanging around in the 1800s, chronicling the demolition of Parcheminerie's shops as medieval Paris continued to be reshaped into Napoleon III's vision of modernity. Historical photos and drawings reveal that the entire street once looked to be as narrow as the graffitied alley, with houses and shops selling wine and liquor. One of the few things to have survived is the old church.

A flamboyant Gothic cathedral with gargoyles and stained glass, Saint Séverin dates to at least the thirteenth century. A sign indicates that it's dedicated to a Saint Séverin who founded an abbey in Switzerland, though it also acknowledges another Séverin—a sixth-century hermit known as Séverin *solitaire,* said to have lived nearby. According to legend he was buried on the grounds, next to my little hotel. An auspicious sign.

Parcheminerie had a certain mystery, thanks to the old church and the sleepy pedestrian alley with its black street lamps and curiosities in the windows. Across the street, in a Louis XV house, was the Abbey Bookshop. Beyond its glass door, stepstools and side tables were piled upside down, concealing a labyrinth of books stacked as tightly as bones in the catacombs.

A torn copy of a page from *Paris Buildings and Monuments* by a Parisian architect taped to a sidelight said the parchment merchants had left by the late-fifteenth century. Next door, seemingly disparate artifacts were propped in a window in front of closed drapes—a straw hat, a lavender plant, an illustration of an electric-blue Buddha with the words *"le guérisseur"* (the healer)—like clues to a mystery. I photographed them as if they had some meaning that would later be revealed, then aimed my iPhone at the hotel. The photo caught my reflection in the dark glass of the door, my phone obscuring my face like the floating green apple in Magritte's *The Son of Man*.

I crossed onto rue Boutebrie, past the row of trees and the motorcycles parked beneath them, turned left at the corner brasserie, out of sight of the little hotel—and became anonymous.

Alone, there's no need for an itinerary. Walk, and the day arranges itself.

The world's first sidewalks appeared around 2000 B.C. in what is now Turkey. But it was in Paris—where there are at least as many styles of wandering (*flânerie, dérive, errance*) as there are the customary cheek kisses (*la bise*)—that the sidewalk became an avenue for pleasure. No need to follow the 1920s-style red METRO sign underground, or climb into the taxi with *"Parisien"* on its rooftop light. From the sidewalk, the best of the city can be had for free. There are flowering courtyards hidden behind painted doors. There's a giant chocolate gorilla in the window of Patrick Roger, a cow on the awning of the *fromager* La Fermette, a red poodle in the window at Hermès. Follow the sidewalk and you may find a Ferris wheel or, on an overcast spring morning, loaves of fat, round bread marked with a "P" in a small brick storefront on rue du Cherche-Midi. On the windows in fanciful script was the family name: *Poilâne*. I went in.

Poilâne bakes heavy loaves of sourdough bread with sea salt from the marshes of Guérande, a medieval town on the west coast of France. Salvador Dalí was a customer (and the rare recipient of Poilâne's bread sculptures). Julia Child brought a film crew there to shoot a lesson in bread making. Yet any passerby can stop in for a loaf, even just a few slices. A saleswoman cut three for me, each as long as my forearm. I pointed at an apple tart and at the crisp, thin sugar cookies known as *punitions* (punishments), sold in a clear bag pinched in the middle, like goldfish at a street market.

I had made it halfway up rue du Cherche-Midi with $17 worth of pastries in a paper sack when the morning mist, which an American in Paris can easily write off as poetic, became rain. The wet bag began to rip. My umbrella busted a rib, and what remained of it was soon flopping around my head like a sunhat.

I walked a few blocks, hunting for some undiscovered coffee shop, before bowing to the inevitable and taking refuge from the rain under the familiar green-and-white umbrellas of Les Deux Magots.

It was a fast storm, blowing in and letting up within minutes, and so from a sidewalk table amid the umbrellas I ordered a café crème and a croque provençal: open-faced slices of toast topped with tomatoes, ham, and a browned dome of grilled cheese.

Les Deux Magots is old Paris. It's not the Paris of South Pigalle or the Haut-Marais, where people line up for empanadas and ice cream at Clasico Argentino, and Glow on the Go! sells beauty products alongside nitro cold-brew coffee and gluten-free avocado toast. The word *"magot,"* as in Les Deux Magots, is also old. It refers to a Chinese- or Japanese-style figurine, not an insect, and there are two in the café, the name of which is taken from the novelty shop that once occupied Les Deux's original location on rue de Buci. The waiter brought over a couple of pitchers—one dark, one light—and zipped away, leaving me alone with my coffee.

The pleasures of mealtime have long involved company. The word "companion" comes from the Old French, *compaignon*, literally "one who breaks bread with another." Indeed, French gastronomy is included on UNESCO's Intangible Cultural Heritage of Humanity List (along with the tango, falconry, and Chinese shadow puppetry), where it's described as a social practice that "emphasizes togetherness."

To share a meal is to undoubtedly experience one of life's great joys. Yet this doesn't mean that there can't be some kind of connection when we eat alone, be it with ourselves, what's around us, or a higher power. UNESCO states that French gastronomy emphasizes "the pleasure of taste," and that some of the essential elements involve utilizing local products, pairing food with wine, and taking the time to smell and taste items at the table. Alone, we can plumb local markets and examine their wares closely. We can breathe in and relish the flavors in a sauce, or the coolness of a pitcher of cream. We don't necessarily take time to do these things in the presence of company, particularly during lively conversation. A solo meal is an opportunity to go slow; to savor.

"Savoring" sounds like it ought to involve an Adirondack chair and a glass (or bottle) of wine. But then one morning on rue des Saints-Pères I watched a man in a suit barrel along the sidewalk, stop abruptly outside a flower shop, stick his nose in a potted pink rose, and inhale before he resumed speeding in my direction. What exactly does it mean to savor? Is it relaxing with a drink? An impromptu pause to enjoy the scent of a flower? And does it just happen, like rain showers and moonrises? Or are there ways to invite it in?

In the last decade, the science of well-being has exploded. Prescriptions for happiness abound, and there's no shortage of studies to refer to. (It's worth noting that many studies demonstrate that while a particular behavior or action may be associated with happiness, the behavior may or may not be the *cause* of that happiness.) Certain strategies, like smiling more, sound like reasonable, if obvious, ideas. Other tactics may work for some personality types, though there is no universal prescription. There are, however, a number of practices widely believed by social scientists to help us flourish.

Savoring is one of them. In the 1980s, Fred B. Bryant and Joseph Veroff felt that there was something missing from existing dimensions of psychological well-being, like happiness and satisfaction. They reasoned that there should be another factor—one that had to do with controlling your own positive experiences. Bryant's empirical research involving engagement and enjoyment ultimately led him to the concept of savoring. In *Savoring: A New Model of Positive Experience,* the scholars define it as "a search for the delectable, delicious, almost gustatory delights of the moment." It describes the *process* of enjoyment: how a person manages or "attends to" not just a gustatory delight, but any kind of positive experience.

It's more than passively taking pleasure in something, Bryant, a professor of psychology at Loyola University Chicago, explains. Savoring is actively aiming for the most joy to be found in a moment. Consider how Apollonia Poilâne, owner of Poilâne and a granddaughter of its founder, describes her favorite spot, the bakehouse—"a simple and quiet place where the heat of the oven envelops you"—and how she engages the moment: "I like to see and perform the baking gestures, it's like a coordinated ballet, and to smell the yeast, touch the kneaded dough . . . One uses the five senses, which perhaps explains the fulfilling feeling one has after having finished baking the batch." In a video of her father making bread in the basement of the shop on rue du Cherche-Midi, he marvels at the beauty of a cracked egg in a circle of flour, then begins tenderly mixing ingredients with one hand, feeling the texture of the butter with the tips of his fingers.

Finding joy in the moment is what Julia Child did when she sat down to her first meal in France—the meal that ignited a passion, a career, and a revolution in American cooking. "I closed my eyes and inhaled the rising perfume," she said of sitting before a platter of sole meunière. "Then I lifted a forkful of fish to my mouth, took a bite, and chewed slowly." It tasted of browned butter and the ocean.

This is what the writer Eleanor Clark is getting at when she describes degustation as not merely about satisfying hunger, but as an activity that involves imagination, taking our time and paying attention—even indulging in a moment of silence before that first bite or sip. Indeed, the French philosopher Jean-Paul Aron tells us that in the nineteenth century the beginning of a meal was eaten in silence, only to be pierced "by the scarcely audible sound of a smile escaping from impatient lips, or the last sighs exhaled by sizzling meats snatched suddenly from the oven."

For a concrete example, consider Tokaido, a French board game. In it, players must travel Japan's ancient Tokaido road along the coast to Kyoto from Tokyo (known as Edo in the period in which the game is set), taking in vistas of mountains, seas, and rice paddies; tasting local specialties; soaking in hot springs; donating coins to temples; and meeting locals. The object of the game, unlike most, is not to get to the end of the road first or amass the most money. It's to have the richest experience possible.

Doing so doesn't come naturally to everyone, particularly when eating, and particularly when what we're eating is from, say, a food plaza off a thruway, not a forkful of sole meunière. But savoring can be learned, and there's good reason to try. People who become skilled at "capturing the joy of the present moment," as the psychologist Sonja Lyubomirsky at the

University of California, Riverside, has written, are also "less likely to experience depression, stress, guilt and shame."

There isn't just one way to go about this. There are many savoring techniques that can be used at any time, in private or in public, alone or with others. But in general, they all have one requirement: that we focus our attention on the present experience. That may sound daunting, but there are specific things we can do to achieve this; everyday actions that are surprisingly simple, quick, and elegant yet can make a big difference in the way we experience the world.

On that spring morning at Les Deux, as people were darting and disappearing around the church of Saint-Germain-des-Prés like billiard balls knocked into motion, carrying tote bags, pushing strollers, heading off to work and school over the wet, gray pavers, into the mouth of the Métro, I slipped a finger through the handle of my coffee cup and eased back in my rattan chair.

To focus on the present moment, Bryant explained, it helps to refrain from certain habits, like multitasking, worrying, latching on to what's wrong or negative, and ruminating about the past or future. Easier said than done. Most of us spend nearly 47 percent of our waking hours each day thinking about something other than what we're doing, according to research by Matthew A. Killingsworth, a Robert Wood Johnson Foundation Health and Society scholar, and Harvard psychologist Daniel T. Gilbert. That matters, the researchers say, because one of the strongest predictors of happiness is whether or not your attention is focused where you are in the present. "People are substantially less happy when their minds are wandering than when they're not," Killingsworth told a crowd at a

TEDxCambridge conference. That's proven to be true, he said, even when our minds wander to things that bring us pleasure, like sex.

Happily, even us mind-wanderers, multitaskers, and ruminators can master ways to savor. One method, particularly useful for travelers, involves what Bryant calls "temporal awareness": reminding ourselves that the moment won't last, that soon the meal will be gone or the trip will end. It may seem counterintuitive, but awareness that something is fleeting tends to increase our enjoyment of it, for as Bryant explained, when time gets scarce, it heightens motivation. It's the truth behind the maxim about only knowing what you've got when it's gone. And one trick to preventing that from happening, Bryant said, is to treat the moment we're in as if it's the last of a lifetime.

To do that, he suggests identifying the sources of joy in the moment by asking ourselves questions like *What is it that is going to be gone? What is the joy in it; the sources of the positive feeling?*

Alone at a sidewalk table in Saint-Germain-des-Prés, just after a June rain, I listen to the low hum of French being spoken around me, breathe in the scent of coffee, feel the breeze across my cheek, in my hair, carrying away the last of the storm; all the things I'll miss when I'm back home.

Like temporal awareness, many savoring techniques can be tried anywhere. One, called "sensory-perceptual sharpening," involves heightening an experience by focusing on just one of your senses—like closing your eyes to fully appreciate the fragrance of a warm baguette, or to better hear the wind rustle the trees.

A wonderful savoring strategy for the start of a trip is what Bryant calls "self-congratulation": reminding yourself of how long you've waited for the moment to happen (you're finally taking that solo vacation!) or why you deserve to be experiencing it (you spent a year saving up for a plane ticket). This "recalled anticipation," Bryant said, is the joy of appreciating an experience that you had been looking forward to. It's how I felt after handing the key to room 61 to the woman at the desk and walking out of the hotel onto an empty street, the whole of Paris waiting.

Absorbing details and taking mental photographs of a moment is another way to savor it—a process Bryant calls "memory building." While this mental snapshot captures a visual record—the green-and-white umbrellas of Les Deux Magots, the steeple of the Romanesque church—it's not meant to be only a panoramic. The aim should be to build into your mental photograph the multisensory feeling of the moment as well: the air redolent with warm rain, the tinkling of porcelain cups being lifted and returned to saucers, the soft *mercis* and *au revoirs*. This way, when you mentally summon an experience, you'll rekindle more than images.

Yet while savoring is fundamentally about the present moment, skilled savorers know how to play across time, choosing particular moments by dipping into the past or even the future. Now and then they may decide to savor through anticipation, recalled anticipation, or by reminiscing (more on that later).

To help embed mental snapshots in his memory, Bryant often begins reminiscing about a trip as soon as possible, sometimes when he's in an airplane seat on the way home. He may start by thinking back to the day before he even left, to packing and setting the alarm. His mind searches for the details: the arrival of the taxi and the song the driver was playing on the radio; those feelings of excitement about what was to come. He tries to relive the trip almost in real time; so much so that he doesn't necessarily get through the whole thing by the time the plane lands.

There is a difference, though, between savoring a moment and clinging to it. There's no scientific upside to clinging, to mourning the last days of a great vacation. Acceptance of this requires practice, but to be a great traveler, to be a good student of life, as Bryant put it, you have to learn to let go. "One of the laws of travel," he said, "one of the laws of the kingdom, is it must end."

Learning to savor many experiences in many different ways is important, Bryant said, because the diversity of savoring strategies in our repertoires is predictive of how much we enjoy the moment—which could explain why my time during the Paris assignment months earlier was so poignant.

It was a happy accident that the things I did in service of that assignment also turned out to be savoring strategies. I was living in the moment, memory building, and using sensory perceptual sharpening, because I knew I'd be writing about the experience later. I wasn't doing the usual worrying because I was away from home and my responsibilities there. I was acutely aware that every moment was fleeting, that I had only one chance to get the story. And I began reminiscing almost as soon as I left for home because I had a deadline. All of these parameters inadvertently allowed me to savor my experience in ways I simply didn't when I was off-duty.

Long after that trip, I learned that Bryant and Veroff had

likened the act of savoring to "taking the perspective of an inquiring journalist toward one's own pleasurable experiences." Turns out, there are advantages to bringing a reporter's habits to daily life.

At the sidewalk tables outside Les Deux, patrons sit across from the church of Saint-Germain-des-Prés, which has existed, at least in part, for a thousand years. Rilke likened the cathedrals in the midst of Paris to a sea or a forest. "They are solitude and stillness," he wrote in a letter to his wife in 1902. "They are the future as they are the past."

People come to Les Deux Magots and its neighbor Café de Flore not necessarily for what the cafés offer today, but for what they used to be: asylums of the great thinkers and artists who worked, socialized, and argued there, including Hemingway, Picasso, Sartre, Simone de Beauvoir, Camus, James Baldwin, and Richard Wright. The coffee may be overpriced, but it's the price of history. At times it was grim: Sartre and de Beauvoir's café days were marked by a scarcity of food, and the horrors of the German occupation. But we don't often think about that while we drink our coffee. We come because Hemingway and Sartre came, because we feel there is something of their spirit there, something that might rub off, something that speaks to who we want to be.

Outside Les Deux, silver kegs were being delivered to the curb along with crates of Perrier and bottles of Badoit. Soon the bottles would be emptied. My chair would be filled by another diner, who knows how many more times that day, or that season. I finished the last of my croque provençal, grateful for my time at the table, for the church, for the coffee, for the morning rain that brought me there.

———

When I returned to room 61 that afternoon, dark clouds were again gathering. Beyond the balcony, over the dome of the Panthéon, they were merging into a sinister band, as purple as the inside of a clam shell.

I reached into the Poilâne bag and tried a couple of punishment cookies as rain began to plop and splash in through the windows, which I had opened wide in anticipation. The streets below were empty; people had already sought shelter when—*swoosh!*

Sitting in that room with the windows open during a rainstorm was like being in a treehouse with a wool blanket. I felt a childish kind of excitement; a longing for thunder. Alone, I could listen to the rain come down, listen to it in a way you can't when someone else is around, with bodily stillness. It fell hard, soaking the streets, scattering the pigeons.

Sometimes during my stay I ate outside on the balcony with the birds that flew in arcs from the church to the chamfered building across the way. There's no shame in occasionally eating in. The food writer M.F.K. Fisher once lounged around her hotel room in Avignon in her pajamas, drinking Champagne. James Beard ordered a Christmas-morning breakfast of buttermilk pancakes with maple syrup, bacon, a bowl of raspberries with sugar and thick cream, and a pot of tea to his hotel room. Breakfast is my favorite meal to take alone; it's just me and the dawn chorus, hot coffee, and a warm croissant.

Around the corner from the hotel, at Marché Maubert, a long-running market in a parking lot, I could pick up fruit. Or buy a glass jar of yogurt with chunks of cherries from the Loire Valley at Laurent Dubois, the *fromager*, where rounds of cheese in paper cupcake liners are decorated like cookies with dark, sticky hearts of fig and nuts. A stop at Eric Kayser on rue Monge for the croissant was essential. I would hurry back to the Hôtel Parc Saint Séverin, butter-stained bag in hand, to fill a glass with water from the bathroom sink and take the *Vogue*s from the closet to the table on the balcony in time for the morning church bells.

Unfailingly, the smoking man would appear in his boxers. In a way, I was more a part of rue de la Parcheminerie on the balcony than on the street. Even if no one on the block was ready for the day or cared to venture out, we could all see one another in our various states of disarray; half-dressed, talking on phones, brushing aside curtains, leaning out dormer windows to see what was happening below. We drank in the quartier from our private places.

The rain fell harder and louder, leaving the zinc roofs glistening. Then a burst of bright white light broke through the clouds, lit up the pale apartment buildings, and made the petals of the red ivy geraniums transparent: an honest-to-goodness sun shower. Little by little, the rain began to hush, slow, become gentler still until—silence.

I cracked the French doors and stepped barefoot onto the soaked wood. A bird flapped its wings. A man sneezed.

A boy rode by on the back wheel of his bicycle.

# La Vie est Trop Courte Pour Boire du Mauvais Vin ~ Life Is Too Short to Drink Bad Wine

*On Eating Alone*

*There's only one very good life, and that's the life that you know you want, and you make it yourself.*

—Diana Vreeland

Comptoir Turenne is on the ground floor of a nineteenth-century building with battered shutters in the Haut-Marais, on the less fashionable end of rue de Turenne. On the more fashionable end, Glow on the Go! serves concoctions like the Lolita with organic cherries and "superfoods adaptogens," Baby Beluga sells bikinis and matching sunglasses for Capri-bound toddlers, and the windows of Delphine Pariente's jewelry shop advise: *Soyez heureux,* be happy.

Comptoir Turenne has no such panache. Its sidewalk views are mainly of a real estate agency and a men's suit shop. It is not on "must-eat" lists. Visitors are not burdened by the ghosts of Hemingway and Sartre to have an indelible experience. All of this makes Turenne a laid-back spot for breakfast *pour un*. You can sit under its cheerful red awnings, mere blocks from the action, and fancy yourself Parisian.

Portions, however, appear to be measured with Americans in mind. A croque madame arrived at the table looking as if it had been flown in from the Cheesecake Factory. A sunny-side-up egg was as big as a pancake. Beneath it, thick, crusty bread was covered in toasted cheese. Beside it, french fries were piled in a little deep-fryer basket. A salad was already beginning to migrate off the plate. There was barely room on the table for my café crème and the speculoos tucked between the cup and saucer.

I eyed the speculoos. The Buddhist monk Thich Nhat Hanh tells a story about being a child and taking half an hour, sometimes forty-five minutes, to finish a cookie that his mother bought him. "I would take a small bite and look up at the sky," he wrote. "Then I would touch the dog with my feet and take another small bite. I just enjoyed being there, with the sky, the earth, the bamboo thickets, the cat, the dog, the flowers."

I can polish off a speculoos in less time than it takes to say "speculoos." Nonetheless, Nhat Hanh's story resonates in an age when it's not unusual for a meal to be eaten with one hand while the other is posting a photo of it to Instagram. Men in suits stopped for coffee and cigarettes. Children were being walked to school. For the solo diner, no view is better than the one from the sidewalk, even the one from Comptoir Turenne. When you're not sitting across from someone, you're sitting across from the world.

I've eaten by myself in France more than anywhere else,

with the exception of my own country where, more than half the time when we're eating, we're eating alone. That's more often than in any previous generation. Pressed for time at work or school, Americans frequently eat by themselves at breakfast and when snacking, according to the NPD Group, a market research company. More than half of lunch meals are solitary. And more than 30 percent of Americans have dinner alone because they're single or on a different schedule from their partner. The trend is being seen in other countries, too. In South Korea, for instance, it's largely being driven by long work hours. And while many may not be dining alone by choice, the fact that more people are doing it is changing perceptions. "Dining alone has not only become socially acceptable in South Korea," Euromonitor reported, noting that Seoul is an incubator for trends that resonate throughout East Asia and beyond, "it is almost fashionable."

Be that as it may, all too often the meals we have alone are rushed and forgotten, as if they didn't matter. In the United States, for instance, dining alone has led to what the Hartman Group, a food and beverage consultancy, has called the "snack-ification of meals." Certainly, we all have times when we have to eat and run, but what about the rest of the time? Why should a meal on our own be uninspired or scarfed down as if consumed on the shoulder of an interstate highway? Why shouldn't the saying *la vie est trop courte pour boire du mauvais vin*—life is too short to drink bad wine—apply, even when we sip alone?

France has its share of fast-food chains. (McDonald's, *McDo* as it's known, is popular.) Still, the French have historically spent more time eating than the people of other nations—more than two hours a day, according to a study by the Organization for Economic Cooperation and Development. Even when time is of the essence, culinary innovators in cities like Paris offer modern twists on international street food and sandwiches with wholesome ingredients that make a quick bite still feel nourishing and laid-back. As the writer Alice B. Toklas said, the French bring to the table "the same appreciation, respect, intelligence and lively interest that they have for the other arts, for painting, for literature and for the theatre." This history of thoughtfully prepared meals and passion for *terroir,* the combination of earth and climate that distinguishes a wine, has made Paris an ideal place to practice the art of savoring.

Eating alone, however, in Paris and beyond, has soured plenty of appetites. Nathaniel Hawthorne cherished his solitude—"It is so sweet to be alone," he wrote to his wife in 1844 while he was in Concord, Massachusetts—but not at mealtime. "I am ashamed to eat alone," he noted in his diary. "It becomes the mere gratification of animal appetite . . . these solitary meals are the dismallest part of my present experience."

Solo dining even prompted the pope to look for company. Vatican tradition had called for the pontiff to eat by himself. But in 1959, during Pope John XXIII's first year as the spiritual ruler, the *Boston Daily Globe* published the headline: "He Shatters Tradition, Refuses to Dine Alone." "I tried it for one week, and I was not comfortable," the pontiff explained. "Then I searched through sacred scripture for something saying I had to eat alone. I found nothing, so I gave it up, and it's much better now."

Through the years, the only thing considered worse than eating alone has been eating alone in public. To borrow a term from the sociologist Erving Goffman, you're a "single," not a "with." In public, a "with," Goffman said, has more protection, choice, and freedom than a "single."

When Steve Martin enters a bustling restaurant in the 1984 film *The Lonely Guy* and tells the captain, "I'm alone," the captain replies, "Alone?" and the entire restaurant—the music, the clattering of cutlery, the blithe chatter—stops. Everyone turns and stares. After a prolonged silence the captain finally says, "Follow me, sir," and a cold spotlight appears on Martin, pursuing him to a table in the center of the crowd, which continues to gawk.

The supposed horror of solo dining was fresh as ever in the 2015 film *The Lobster*. In a world where humans who don't find mates are turned into animals, single people are gathered in a hotel ballroom and made to watch propaganda skits including one called "Man eats alone." The man gets something caught in his throat, chokes, and dies. In a subsequent skit, "Man eats with woman," the man again begins to choke—but this time there's a woman across the table who performs the Heimlich maneuver and saves his life. The audience applauds.

Anxiety about how others perceive us is apparently so outsized that a group of researchers devised a name for it, inspired by the table-for-one ordeal in *The Lonely Guy*: the Spotlight Effect. "People overestimate the extent to which their actions and appearance are noted by others," Thomas D. Gilovich, a professor of psychology at Cornell University, and colleagues wrote in the *Journal of Personality and Social Psychology*. They reached that conclusion following a series of studies about appearance and behavior, one of which asked participants to wear a T-shirt with either a flattering or a potentially embarrassing image and predict how much attention they might attract. In another study, participants were asked to take part in a group discussion and estimate how prominent their positive and negative comments were to others in the group.

In one T-shirt study, subjects wore a shirt showing someone with whom they were happy to be associated, such as Bob Marley or Martin Luther King, Jr. In a different study, participants wore a shirt they felt had a potentially embarrassing image on it: a close-up of Barry Manilow's head. Setting aside the question of whether Mr. Manilow was unjustly categorized, researchers found that the participants in both studies allowed their own focus on the shirt to distort their predictions of how much attention it would garner.

Similar results were found in a study involving subjects taking part in a group discussion: When evaluating their contributions to the discussion, they overestimated the prominence of their own statements to the rest of the group. "An 'obvious' social gaffe on a first date, an awkward stumble at the front of a line, or the misreading of a crucial passage of a prepared speech—each may seem shameful and unforgettable to us," the researchers said, "but they often pass without notice by others."

Does this same principle apply to dining solo?

Bella DePaulo, a social scientist and academic affiliate with the department of psychological and brain sciences at the University of California, Santa Barbara, had already gone in search of answers. To evaluate perceptions of solo diners she and colleagues at the University of Virginia in Charlottesville had four twentysomethings (two men and two women) and four fortysomethings (two men and two women) visit a restaurant and be photographed. The pictures were then Photoshopped to create a variety of situations: Each participant was made to look as if he or she was dining alone, or with a person of the other sex, or with a person of the same sex. The researchers used Photoshop, instead of simply having the diners rearrange themselves in different scenarios, so that each person's facial expression and posture would remain the same in each photo, regardless of whether that person appeared to be eating alone or with others. This was important, DePaulo explained, to ensure that the diners would not be judged differently because of shifting postures or expressions.

She and her colleagues then took the photos to an area shopping mall and asked hundreds of adults there to look at a particular person in one of the photos and tell them why they thought that person was out to dinner. If the photo featured someone dining solo, the researchers asked the shoppers why they thought the person was having dinner alone. Some of the respondents said things like, "He is lonely" and "She looks depressed." Others said positive, even wistful, things such as, "Enjoying a few good peaceful moments" and "He is secure."

When respondents observed the photos of the pairs, there were negative interpretations (the couple went to dinner "to have a talk because their relationship needs some mending" or they wanted to "get away from the children") and positive ones (the man was having "dinner with his wife for fun" and "they enjoy spending time together").

DePaulo, a leading researcher and author about single life, didn't publish the findings in a scientific journal. Why? Because what people thought of the solo diners proved to be no differ-ent than what they thought of the diners who had company, a null result as DePaulo called it, which she felt wouldn't be of interest to journals. Age, the number of diners, and whether they were of the same or opposite sex made no difference.

"We never in a million years thought that we would not find any differences," she explained. When she began her research she figured that people considering dining alone would worry that others might view them as "losers." "It's not that solo din-ers are never dissed," she said. "But when people look at couples in restaurants, they're also saying equally dismissive things."

So why dismiss yourself?

A sidewalk brasserie like Comptoir Turenne is an easy place to begin. Anything goes; sneakers, T-shirts, pinstripe suits. You don't have to be escorted to a table. Pick one you like and take a seat. Café tables are small; you never feel as if someone is missing. Look around and you'll notice that others are also eat-ing alone, taking the morning at their own pace.

Years ago, when I began dining out solo, I often ate fast food. The price was right, and I didn't fret about the court of public opinion in a McDonald's, where it's common for people to eat by themselves. (Besides, I happen to like McDonald's; you can learn a thing or two about a city by observing the goings-on there.) Yet that generally meant forgoing better nutrition and opportunities to experience homemade regional cuisine, hos-pitality, and ambience. And so I began eating alone at cheerful local places instead, often at brunch, lunch, or at around 6:30, before prime dinnertime. For my entire life I've been hungry for dinner at an hour people said was befitting octogenarians.

Alone, I could be the eighty-year-old I always wanted to be. (Mind you, in the early nineteenth century, dinner traditionally began at 5 p.m. It wasn't until the end of the century that 8 p.m. became the norm, and then only for galas.)

Meal by meal, I began to try better restaurants. I made a point of learning how to ask, *"Avez-vous une table pour une?"* ("Do you have a table for one?"), which seemed to win points with hosts and hostesses alike. Meals at museum restaurants were also an easy introduction. Today, a number of them offer food so good it's tempting to visit the museum just to dine there. (Le Frank at the Fondation Louis Vuitton is an example. Jean-Louis Nomicos, the Michelin-starred chef there, offers terrific contemporary French lunchtime fare in a bright glass corner near a path through the Bois de Boulogne.) These lunches and early dinners are not only a genuine pleasure but are also practical: Ordering from lunch or all-day menus at nicer restaurants typically costs less. And eating earlier makes it easier to get a table at popular places whose evening time slots may be booked months in advance.

I'm shy, and while I was mildly concerned about what people might think of me when I began dining alone, I was more concerned about what *I* might think of me if I didn't try. I didn't want to be someone who experienced less of a city, less of life, because I was afraid. So I went.

By dining out, even at less than stellar places, I experienced more of whatever city I was in—practicing my terrible French on patient waiters and cashiers, sampling unfamiliar dishes, observing locals, figuring out where I was in relation to everything else. On rue de Turenne, for example, is the Saint-Claude bus stop, from which the hit song "Saint-Claude" by the French pop star Christine and the Queens gets its name. People step off the bus; lounge on the grass in the Place des Vosges; walk through the garden of the seventeenth-century Hôtel de Sully with its tidy box shrubs to the sound of birds and a nearby harpist. Beyond it are the gates of the oldest covered food market in Paris, the Marché des Enfants Rouges, where locals buy apricots and cheese, baguettes and butter, sunflowers and roses. Some stop by Le Traiteur Marocain, where a man with a couple of whisks tends to a pyramid of couscous; others stand in line for galettes and sandwiches that smell like heaven.

To eat out alone is to partake of such experiences. And if you happen to be a woman dining alone, you also happen to be exercising a hard-won right, one that still doesn't exist everywhere. "It was impossible for a woman to go about alone," Virginia Woolf wrote of Jane Austen in *A Room of One's Own*. "She never travelled; she never drove through London in an omnibus or had luncheon in a shop by herself." Indeed, generations of women simply weren't allowed to dine alone in restaurants and bars. As late as the beginning of the twentieth century, New Yorkers were debating legislative bills about whether women should be allowed to eat out without a male escort. And it wasn't just men who wanted to keep the status quo. "I believe it is a protection to all decent women that women alone should not be allowed to eat in public restaurants," said a member of the Women's Republican Club in 1908, according to the *New York Times*. Despite the objection, the club passed a resolution favoring a bill that would allow women to dine in public places without a male escort. Doing so, however, continued to be difficult, not for a little while, but for decades. As one restaurateur told the *Times* in 1964: If a "good-looking lady without a partner asks for a table, you wonder why she is alone and I've had my experience with that situation!" It wasn't uncommon for women alone to be presumed to be like the women in paintings by Van Gogh and Manet—prostitutes.

Things weren't much better in 1970. A *New York* magazine article that year began: "In this most liberal of cities, a woman has no legally guaranteed right to enter a restaurant." When Mother Courage, the country's first feminist restaurant (according to the Greenwich Village Society for Historic Preservation), opened two years later, it provided a place for solo female diners to tuck in. "A woman coming to eat here alone knows she won't feel like a freak and won't get hassled by men," Dolores Alexander, who founded the restaurant with her partner, Jill Ward, told *People* magazine in 1975. Even today women are still reporting the same problems experienced by Alexander's generation.

Yet despite decades of unwanted attention and articles depicting eating alone as some frightful activity, women have long cherished a solitary meal. M.F.K. Fisher, who wasn't immune to feeling self-conscious when dining out by herself, could wax poetic about its pleasures. Fellow food writer Marion Cunningham, a champion of family mealtime, also appreciated solo dining: "Sometimes eating supper alone feels private, quiet, and blessedly liberating," she wrote in her popular *Supper Book*, where she devoted a page to "Supper Alone." There she briefly extolls the sorts of unconventional meals that can be enjoyed alone (she liked a baked potato with olive oil and coarse pepper and salt, followed by vanilla ice cream) as well as the opportunity to cook something restorative (for her, it was split pea soup). In 2017, the *New York Times* asked the humorist Fran Lebowitz which three writers she would invite to a literary dinner party. "None," she replied. "My idea of a great literary dinner party is Fran, eating alone, reading a book."

Now and then people decry reading at the table as "cheating," as if it's somehow not truly dining alone. Obviously we don't want to be mindlessly putting food into our mouths while focusing on our reading, but as anyone who has ever lingered over a meal knows, both are experiences that can be savored together. For those just beginning to travel solo or dine solo, a book is a terrific companion. And for those who simply love to read, alone time at the table may be their only opportunity to do so in the course of a day.

I get pleasure just from watching others alone with their books, be it at Comptoir Turenne or KB CaféShop on Avenue Trudaine, where you can sit at a communal wood table or, as I did, on a stool facing the street in the open shopfront. Here, a man escorts his poodle past a newsstand. There, a handful of people with cameras and tripods arrive for a fashion shoot beside an unloved merry-go-round.

Once considered the purview of business travelers, dining solo has become a significant part of leisure travel, as well as of everyday life. In the United States reservations for parties of one grew by more than 60 percent in 2015 over the previous two years, according to OpenTable, the online restaurant reservations company. Solo dining has increased across Europe and in parts of Asia, too.

The atmosphere of cities is beginning to change as more people who live alone eat out and gravitate to solo-friendly concepts like "groceraunts" (in-store dining in places like Whole Foods and Cojean), Euromonitor has found. At Ichiran, the Japanese ramen chain, solo diners can seat themselves in private "flavor concentration booths" with dividers and bamboo shades that separate them from the waiters, enabling guests to focus on the taste and smell of the food. "Our goal is for diners to understand and appreciate solo dining, dining without speaking a word to the employees, dining just between you, yourself, and the food in front of you," says Hana Isoda, Ichiran's former director of marketing and business development, in a video for Zagat.com. Andy Warhol, who said he liked eating alone and wrote about wanting to start a restaurant chain where people could sit in booths and watch television, would have been tickled by the concept.

Today, some restaurants are aiming to attract solo diners by giving them the screen time Warhol craved, offering free wi-fi, charging outlets, and tablets for use during a meal, which is convenient for travelers who need to charge their phones or look up directions, though it's not particularly conducive to savoring. On the other end of the spectrum is Eenmaal, a temporary restaurant that was opened by Marina van Goor in Amsterdam in 2013. Each table sat only one, and there was no wi-fi. Guests came alone, ate alone, and were encouraged to disconnect: read magazines and books, sketch, write, or simply enjoy the food and music. "At Eenmaal," van Goor said in a talk for the lecture series CreativeMornings Amsterdam, "you are your own company." Her words echoed those uttered more than two centuries ago by the composer Haydn, who once told a hotel waiter to serve him a dinner that some contended could have fed five. The waiter, according to the *Boston Daily Globe* in 1889, said, "But, sir, the company is not come."

Haydn replied: "Pooh! de gompany! I am de gompany!"

Paris is among the most appealing places to be your own company. It was there that the *New Yorker* food writer A.J. Liebling said he learned the art of eating. "I was often alone, but seldom lonely," he wrote in *Between Meals,* his memoir of his days in Paris. "I enjoyed the newspapers and books that were my usual companions at the table."

Under the red awnings of Comptoir Turenne, the men on either side of me—one in skinny jeans and baby-blue Converse sneakers; the other in a suit and tie—lit after-breakfast cigarettes. Tourists wandered by in the direction of the Picasso Museum, area art galleries, and Merci, where shoppers line up in an industrial warehouse to buy necessities of modern life, like Bluetooth headsets, pink computer glasses, and soap made from tomato leaves.

To sit outside a Paris café at breakfast is to observe the city as it wipes the sleep from its eyes: the soft clink of a cup and saucer, the turning of newspaper pages, the passerby with a cigarette who asks for a light, and me at my little round table, nibbling a speculoos, sipping my café crème.

# A Picnic for One in the Luxembourg Gardens

*Alternatives to the Table*

*Even the simplest of picnics can be a delight. All it takes is the right state of mind and a place to settle.*

—James Beard, *The Armchair James Beard*

The Marché Raspail arrives each week under the trees on an island on Boulevard Raspail.

Colorful tarps shield long tables of olives, onions, and fish from the sun. A woman shows off straw totes from Madagascar while girls with bouquets of spring flowers call out to passersby. A seller greeted me "*bonjour*" and extended an arm over tubs of dates, pistachios, and macadamia nuts. In his hand, an aluminum scoop held a toasted almond from Greece on its tip. I plucked it up and placed it in my mouth. It was covered in a fine, flavorful dust of salt.

A meal alone doesn't have to take place at a restaurant table. Rather, it can be enjoyed while wandering a weekly market like the Raspail. It can be taken while strolling a street like rue des Martyrs in the 9th arrondissement, where sex shops have given way to cheesemongers and you can still gawk, though not at peep shows, but at pâtisserie windows with baba au rhum and Framboisine. And when it's spring in Paris, a solitary meal can—and should—be taken in the Luxembourg Gardens.

But first: provisions.

To my novice eye, nearly all of the fruit stalls at the Marché Raspail looked the same. Rule #1 of market shopping: When in doubt, follow the nearest Frenchwoman. I trailed a pair in loose white blouses as they snaked through the crowd with their totes, passing stall after stall of perfectly attractive produce, all the way to the bespectacled man in the many-pocketed vest.

His head was shorn. His sleeves were rolled. He flitted from makeshift troughs of pears, peaches, and grapes to a scale and back again, pulling bills out of his vest, jamming coins into his pockets, scooping *fraises des bois* and dark Starking cherries into paper sacks. It was a brisk business. I waited my turn, listening intently to the women ahead of me so as to correctly pronounce *cerise* and *fraise*.

As the customer in front of me left, the man in the vest leaned over the bin of cherries, combing through them with bare hands and the precision and speed of a machine, snapping up the bruised berries and tossing them over his shoulder. When at last he looked at me, I opened my mouth—and became Marcel Marceau. I pointed at the cherries and little strawberries. (Rule #2 of market shopping: Learn how to say "this one"—*celui-ci*—and "that one"—*celui-là*—which allows for communication in a variety of situations.) He was unfazed and filled to the brim a couple of squat paper sacks decorated with simple drawings of fruit and the words "*Passion*" and "*Santé*," Passion and Health.

I paid, took the bags, and shadowed another Frenchwoman to a nearby cheese stall where she was buying glass jars of yogurt from Normandy. Each one had little stars on top arranged in the shape a green leaf, which I subsequently found out is the "Euro-leaf" symbol, used in the European Union to identify products where at least 95 percent of the agricultural ingredients are organic.

Rule #3: Be curious. Curiosity—about a salty almond or a jar of yogurt—can turn eating into an investigation, transforming the experience of doing it alone. It then becomes about more than just satisfying an appetite. It's an opportunity to practice a foreign language, discover where and how something is made, or simply appreciate an artful display. It's a chance to try something new—for instance, at the chocolatier Jacques Genin you can learn that caramels aren't necessarily plasticky cubes; they can be soft treats in flavors like blackcurrant and rhubarb—and to find out about local customs and honors like the M.O.F., *Meilleurs Ouvriers de France,* a title awarded by the French government to the country's best craftsmen. Winners, like the *fromager* Laurent Dubois, often advertise the distinction in their windows or on their awnings, which can be handy guideposts for hungry travelers.

Opportunities to learn about the art of eating, the art of living, are all around, like at the cheesemonger Marie-Anne Cantin on rue du Champ de Mars, where wheels of Coulommiers, Époisses, and Olivet cendré—some as big as birthday cakes—are piled on wooden blocks and risers amid bowls of wine bottles on ice, and jars of black cherry and apple jelly. I once spent a morning boulangerie-hopping, visiting previous winners of the city's annual best baguette contest—*Grand Prix de la Baguette*—to find out what victory tastes like. As with a lavish meal in nineteenth-century France, the experience wasn't strictly about eating, or stirring the senses. It was also a matter of edification, "a sincere desire to learn, to taste, to appreciate," as Aron put it.

I stepped up to the counter at the Marché Raspail and asked for a glass of *citron* (lemon) yogurt, to which the young man working there said something in French that I didn't catch. Figuring he might be asking if I wanted a spoon, I answered *oui*.

I guessed right. Rule #4: Enjoy *petites victoires*.

About a seven-minute walk later, I arrived at the tall black gates of the Luxembourg Gardens. I carried *Passion* and *Santé* to the edge of a leafy promenade dappled with midmorning sun. Green metal chairs were facing every which way, like cows in a pasture. I pulled two together: one for me; one for my parcels.

Berries peeked over the tops of each sack. They looked so beautiful in the sunlight, I thought it a kind of pity to eat them.

The thought passed. I widened the mouth of the bags in the quiet company of strangers on their own garden chairs, some in the sun, some in the shade, reading or taking in the view on the outskirts of the action, away from the Medici fountain with its garlands of ivy, and the sunbathers ringing the pond. I tried not to eat the cherries as if they were M&Ms. I considered where they might have been before the man in the vest scooped them into the crinkly bag, what the farm they came from looked like, how the sun must have warmed them on the trees. They were so deep in color that had I posted them to Instagram, people would have assumed I used a filter.

The Luxembourg Gardens were built for Marie de' Medici, wife of Henri IV, to recall the Boboli Gardens of her native Florence. And there I was, inviting myself for breakfast, dragging a tiny spoon over the top of my yogurt, skimming each white layer, down into the glass jar. It was tart, tasting of a real lemon. Across the dusty lane, a man in a low-slung chair was minding a public toilet, collecting euros in a cupped hand between drags of a cigarette. The wind blew the leaves, and the sun moved this way and that. Before long I was scraping the last of the yogurt from its jar. I reached for the lid to see the name of the maker so I'd be able to find it again, and there, in pale orange letters, was my own name: *Les Fromages de Stéphanie*.

Laws of probability can account for this coincidence; I hardly have an unusual name. Any delight at seeing it was likely what psychologists call implicit egotism: the tendency to prefer things—like names—associated with ourselves. Even so, it felt like a wink from the universe, a small sign in the absence of familiar touchstones that I was in the right place, that everything was as it should be.

A friend once remarked that it's through serendipitous encounters with objects and strangers that the world speaks to us. But we have to be listening. In fact, research by Sanda Erdelez, an information scientist at the University of Missouri, suggests that serendipity isn't necessarily a fluke—we can create situations that are conducive to it.

While some people look at the world through a narrow lens,

others are what she calls "super-encounterers." They describe themselves as curious, with a desire for exploration and an interest in different hobbies and subjects, qualities that Erdelez found may have helped make them prone to serendipity. Certainly, many scientists have described the role chance has played in their discoveries. The classic yellow Post-it note, for example, was born of attempts to create a strong adhesive that fell short. And its original yellow color was not part of some grand design: It was the only scrap paper that happened to be on hand.

Super-encounterers not only get excited about encountering information, Erdelez wrote, they may also be more sensitive than others to noticing information in their environment. Think of them as good detectives. In fact, the origins of the word "serendipity" are tied to the detective story. In 1754, when Horace Walpole, a British politician, was writing to his friend and distant cousin about his tendency to find whatever he wanted "wherever I dip for it," he called it "Serendipity." It was a word he said he coined after a fairy tale called "The Travels and Adventures of Three Princes of Serendip."

"As their Highnesses travelled," Walpole wrote, "they were always making discoveries, by accidents and sagacity, of things which they were not in quest of." (This was not really how the fairy tale went, but it was nonetheless Walpole's recounting of it.) Thus the origins of the word "serendipity" lie in clues, "keen observations," and "Sherlock Holmesian insights," as the sociologist Robert K. Merton and Elinor Barber, a research associate, put it in *The Travels and Adventures of Serendipity*, a deep dive into the word's etymology.

Maybe it's not surprising, then, that my own serendipitous moments tend to happen when I'm alone, with time to indulge my curiosity. When I booked a room at the Hôtel Parc Saint Séverin, I had no idea it was on a street that was once known as the street of writers, or that there had been a solitary hermit who lived nearby and was possibly buried next door. And I might never have known had I not taken the time to go down the proverbial rabbit hole.

Or consider the day, back when I was in Paris on the assignment for the *Times,* that I got turned around and wound up beside the gardens of the Musée de Cluny. It was a chilly, wet afternoon, not the sort you care to spend outdoors. But I was feeling tired and figured I'd make the most of being lost by having a look around. Along the perimeter, posters in wood shadowboxes described the garden's features. I made my way down the path, reading each one until I reached the last and noticed something in the right-hand corner.

It was a French detective novel, wrapped in plastic. I looked over my shoulder to see if anyone was watching. There weren't many people around, and the few who were there were reading, spaced out on a long wooden bench, like birds on a wire. I turned my attention back to the mysterious book. Taped to its front was a sticker, about the size of a postage stamp, of a yellow book with spindly arms and legs, speed-walking above a web address: BookCrossing.com.

Years earlier, I had read a blurb about BookCrossing, a community of bibliophiles whose mission is to hide ("release" in BookCrosser parlance) books in "the wild" for others to find and enjoy. I thought the likelihood of ever finding one of their books was infinitesimal. But chance brought us together in a garden more than 3,600 miles from home, in a place I found by being lost.

I looked again to my right and left, reluctant to even touch the book as I was vaguely concerned that I was being poetically framed for petty theft. But the BookCrossing sticker offered reassurance. On second thought, it was more than that: It was an invitation. I picked the book up and exited the garden down a sunken lane between low stone walls, amid ferns and gillyflowers, rejoining the strangers on the sidewalk, each going his own way.

As I walked I occasionally glanced down appreciatively at the novel in my hands, as if I had just made off with a museum artifact. And I felt a gentle tether to the universe which, in that moment, seemed benevolent and maybe not so chaotic after all.

The book was titled *L'affaire est close, The Case Is Closed,* a French translation of the British writer Patricia Wentworth's 1937 novel. I would later learn that the heroine, Miss Maud Silver, was a single female sleuth. Like Agatha Christie's Miss Marple, she was one of the first ever written. Had I been in the garden with someone, I might never have spied the book in the corner. Even if I had, a companion might have quashed my romantic ideas about serendipity. Alone, I was the narrator of my own detective story. By learning to be alert for clues in "ordinary outer life," as the psychologist Marie-Louise von Franz put it in her section of Jung's *Man and His Symbols,* "one is suddenly caught up in an exciting inner adventure."

Whatever the adventure, I always seemed to somehow end up in the Luxembourg Gardens, as if it exerted a gravitational pull. I would be in the neighborhood looking for a place to get coffee and find myself walking through its gates to discover a string orchestra under a canopy of trees, spectators gathered around the bandstand, lost in private thoughts, the music providing cover for their daydreams. Or I would be walking along rue Bonaparte, past the statue of a woman under the big hat, *Sous le Chapeau*, and realize I was only a block from the Gardens. Had I my own hat, I would have tipped it in her direction, one solo traveler to another.

Walking alone in a city that's not my own, I think of what Virginia Woolf wished for the women in Cambridge who came to hear her speak in 1928. "By hook or by crook, I hope that you will possess yourselves of money enough to travel and to idle," she said, "to contemplate the future or the past of the world, to dream over books and loiter at street corners and let the line of thought dip deep in the stream."

# Of Oysters and Chablis

*Servings of Delight and Disappointment*

*Perfectionism never quite works out.*
—Julia Child

On warm spring evenings the sidewalks of Odéon brim with people at tables under awnings and café lights, around a grassy triangle formed by three streets that share a name: Carrefour de l'Odéon. Over here are the pink and black awnings of Le Comptoir du Relais Saint-Germain. Over there, the red café tables of Les Éditeurs. Black umbrellas sprout from the shortest street, outside Le Hibou, where diners can order sardines from Spain and grilled bread with Bordier butter.

Almost all the rattan chairs face the grassy island, like seats at a theater in the round. Everyone can see and be seen, and the *flâneur* can watch "the river of life flow past him in all its splendour and majesty," as Baudelaire put it.

I dashed across the island to an empty chair outside Les Éditeurs beside a man with an espresso and an ashtray filled with cigarette butts. Les Éditeurs isn't known for its food, which was just fine. I was planning to have a light dinner at Le Comptoir, or at the newer spot next door serving small plates at a stand-up bar. But first, some Chablis. And for that, Les Éditeurs was a delightful spot to roost.

The waiter brought over little bowls of peanuts and green and black olives that I speared with a toothpick as bicycles and motorcycles whizzed by. Across the island at Le Comptoir, people were already elbow-to-elbow at round black tables; eating, gesticulating, clinking glasses, tilting their heads back in laughter. A silent movie. I fingered the throat of my wineglass, and the night descended, gentle and mild.

When I was on the assignment for the *New York Times*, I had a salmon and wasabi dish at Le Comptoir that was so good I considered breaking a personal travel rule about never eating in the same place twice. From my chair across the street, I relived that meal, this time with omniscience, knowing all that would come to pass: that I would return to Paris, that I would begin dating the man who is now my husband, that I would see the tulips again.

Before I left for that assignment, I had gone around to various friends and colleagues and assembled a makeshift guide to the city based on the places, bistros, and brasseries they enjoyed most. More than one had said to stop by Le Comptoir. Those conversations didn't just offer ideas and boost my anticipation— they were so warm and wide-ranging that it wouldn't have mattered if I'd never ended up boarding a plane. As my friends spoke, I could see in their eyes that they were doing their own time-traveling, returning to Paris—walking some street, standing on the doorstep of some café, *Oh now, what was the name?*

Later, thousands of miles away in some brasserie where they had once dined, I thought of them. And thus they were, despite appearances to the contrary, at the table with me.

Among the friends who have shared tables and advice are David and Susan Liederman. For them, eating alone was never fraught. David, a chef, restaurateur, and the founder of David's Cookies, frequently dined by himself in France in the 1960s, the golden age of three-star Michelin dining. "I decided I was going to go to every three-star restaurant I could go to, with or without companionship," he explained. "I didn't care. Most of the time it was without anybody. When I used to tell people I did this stuff, they didn't believe it, because who would go to France by themselves, eat by themselves in three-star restaurants?"

But he knew that fine dining with others could get in the way of the experience. You had to listen and talk instead of watch what was going on in the dining room, which he described as nothing short of a finely tuned theatrical production. He would sit at Troisgros in Roanne, France, observing as other customers paid no attention to the scene unfolding in front of them, from the choreography of serving the food, to what was on the plate itself. They would take a bite and then light a cigarette.

"It made me insane," Liederman said. "I wanted to say, 'Open your eyes!'"

For him, eating at Troisgros was, as he once put it, "a sort of spiritual revolution." He recalled a meal there in 1969 after which the waiters brought around trays of pastries, cookies, puddings, and an ice cream cart. "My eyeballs were just spinning in my head watching this whole scene," he said. When the waiters reached his table, he told the captain that he wanted to try a little bit of everything. The captain smiled, moved another table next to Liederman's, and proceeded to set out some thirty desserts.

"To this day," Liederman said, "that's one of the high points of my life." He was in his twenties at the time but had, as the *New York Times* food critic Craig Claiborne wrote of him, "a notably keen sense of perception," and went from being an appreciator to an apprentice to *chef de partie* at Troisgros.

Things have changed. Notably prices. But the tricks to having a good time on your own still apply.

"You don't plop down in one of these good restaurants and whip out your computer and start playing and being oblivious to what's going on around you," Liederman said. "They will respect you if you seem to be taking in the act unfolding in front of you." Even better: Ask to see the kitchen. "Because that means you're really interested in the food," Liederman explained, "and the chef will a) know you're alive, and b) look out for you when you go eat in the restaurant and probably send you something even though he doesn't have to."

"It's different than just coming in, dropping your coat off at the coat check, ordering a martini, and putting your face into a bowl," he continued. "It's showing interest in what the restaurant's doing. And that breaks down a lot of barriers."

"I don't know any chef that wouldn't welcome you into the kitchen. It's almost a given that they're going to be receptive to your asking." And if you like wine, he said, "ask to see the wine cellar. They love showing off their dusty bottles."

Susan Liederman, who has some thirty years of experience owning, running, and buying wine for restaurants in New York (plus years of eating out all over the world), also traveled alone in France, dining in two- and three-star restaurants, "so I know just how well a lone female diner can be treated!" she said.

"It was love of food, love of travel, and I wasn't afraid," she explained of her choice to travel and eat solo. When making a reservation to dine alone at nicer restaurants, she advises telling the person on the phone how much you're looking forward to dining there and thank them for the reservation. When you arrive for your meal, show your enthusiasm, saying something as simple as, "I've looked forward to being here," particularly because a lot of chefs consider it a compliment when someone decides to dine alone at a fine restaurant.

For something more casual, she recommends restaurants with bars or communal tables—like La Régalade or Willi's Wine Bar in the 1st arrondissement. All kinds of restaurants today have counter seating around open kitchens, be it Le Pain Quotidien or L'Atelier de Joël Robuchon Saint-Germain. Another option, she said, is a cooking class. (See the Tips and Tools guide at the back of this book.) And while she's not opposed to "le room service," as a hotel I once stayed in put it, for vegging out and movie watching, she doesn't like to think of travelers routinely grabbing fast food and eating in their rooms out of hesitation to venture out alone. "There's an element of punishing yourself in that," she said, "like 'I'm not worth sitting and having a nice meal.'"

The evening was warm, and as I finished the last of the wine at Les Éditeurs, so was I. I put a few euros on the red table and crossed the street back to the grassy island and the stand-up bar at L'Avant Comptoir de la Mer, which was new since I was last in Paris.

There was a food counter along the sidewalk and inside, a bar that faced polished wine refrigerators. Guests ordered from small boards, each with a plate and a price, that hung from S-hooks on the ceiling. *Adorable!* you think when you see them, though you must then contemplate dinner with your neck in a position better suited for an evening at the planetarium. I ordered by pointing skyward at a photo of what appeared to be fried shrimp balls.

The place was appealing: bright and open to the street. And it was created by the chef behind Le Comptoir, Yves Camdeborde, and where the salmon had been transcendent.

Alas, the shrimp balls, which turned out to be sea urchins, were not. Standing at a bar for dinner ought to make for solo-friendly dining. It's casual, you're facing bartenders, and there are other people beside you, all of which seem conducive to conversation. But I didn't speak enough French to engage anyone, and in any case, the other patrons were occupied with partners or children. At Les Éditeurs, I had had a cold Chablis and a view. Yet I had been so intent on sticking to my plan and trying the latest place that I went and left a good thing behind. I could feel my mood dampening.

Happily, there are other advantages to standing while eating: It's easy to leave. I paid the bill and went next door to the crêperie stand at L'Avant Comptoir, yet another spot owned by Yves Camdeborde. Inside, a chalkboard menu listed sweet offerings like chocolate, banana, and Grand Marnier, for 2 to 3.50 euros. Supplements like honey, orange blossom, and whipped cream were another 50 euro cents each. I ordered a sugar and butter crepe. The cook smiled and nodded, gently swirling batter on a griddle until the pancake was ready. He folded it into a neat triangle, tucked it in paper, and passed it over the counter.

Out on the sidewalk, I bit in and began a slow walk back toward my hotel, past the shop selling flat-caps and straw hats with sashes, and the florist with pots and baskets of cherry tomatoes, lavender, and purple mophead hydrangeas on tables beside the door. And as I walked I felt happy again, high on a mixture of sugar and butter, and the gaiety of Paris on a spring evening.

As I neared the hotel, my balcony came into view with its pink café chairs, as pale as cotton candy. I retrieved the tasseled key from the desk, passed the blue sitting room where in the evenings wine bottles replaced the pastries, and walked up the corkscrew stairs to room 61. I took a wineglass from the closet and swung open the door to the balcony.

Long after my drink at Les Éditeurs, I came across an old review in *Time Out Paris*. The magazine had described the restaurant as relaxed and down-to-earth, "with a mixed clientele tending to solo Americans of a certain age reading novels over a glass of wine." And to think I had had a delightful time! Had someone told me that I would be one of those wine-drinking solo Americans, I would have responded with appropriate chagrin. I might never have slid into a chair at Les Éditeurs or thought about the meal at Le Comptoir and marveled at all that had transpired in the months since. I wouldn't have enjoyed my Chablis. In my ignorance, I had a wonderful time. If only life were always like that. If only we didn't know what we were supposed to be embarrassed by.

Out on the balcony I poured some cheap Sauvignon Blanc that I had picked up at a neighborhood grocery, sat down in the fading light, and took a sip. It was terrible.

But I had the sky. I had the soft sounds of French conversations drifting up from tables outside the fondue restaurant below. I had the breeze on the back of my neck, and the sweep of gray and orange rooftops as the lights of the Eiffel Tower came on.

———

Rue Montorgueil is a wide pedestrian thoroughfare in the 2nd arrondissement lined with cheese, fish, and flower shops. Crates of peaches, apples, grapes, cantaloupes, watermelons, asparagus, and tomatoes are interspersed with restaurant supply stores and café chairs as colorful as the produce.

At Maison Collet, pink pastries in cupcake papers were fashioned to look like little pigs with squiggly tails, with a few erudite piglets wearing chocolate-rimmed glasses. At L'Éclair de Génie, one of several shops to specialize in a single product, éclairs were decorated with polka dots, swirls, leaves, and berries, like 1960s frocks. Some had glossy electric hues and flavors like Cassis, Ananas, and Passion Framboise. At Stohrer, one of the oldest pastry shops in Paris, I stopped in to try the puits d'amour, which I'd read somewhere was enjoyed by Queen Elizabeth II (Stohrer's website features a video of her in a blue, wide-brimmed hat climbing out of a Bentley on rue Montorgueil). This, alas, seemed to have made them popular. "A *demain*," said the man behind the counter. They were sold out until tomorrow.

Just north of all this temptation is Frenchie to Go, a tiny restaurant and takeout joint. Tall, hinged panes of glass open onto a quiet street paved with setts. Customers can eat on sidewalk stools facing a narrow counter into the restaurant, or inside looking out onto rue du Nil. The menu is on blackboards above the register: hot dog, lobster roll, Reuben sandwich, pastrami on rye, fish and chips, to name a few. Tomato-red business cards at the counter that read "Who the fuck is Reuben?!" explain the popular choice to visitors, but I just couldn't get excited about corned beef. "Fish and chips, to go," I said to the tattooed man with the shaved head behind the register.

He asked if I really wanted the order to go—a peculiar question, given the name of the place. But he could see that I wanted to stay.

Not that it mattered. There wasn't an empty chair. I looked around at the people at communal tables and counters eating meat sandwiches and fish from Poissonnerie Terroirs d'Avenir across the street, and then back at the tattooed man. Behind him, men in blue aprons were moving about the open kitchen. He leaned over the counter, surveyed the room, and then pointed at a customer standing against a nearby table. "That man's just waiting on his to-go order," he said in English.

It was a tall round table with a couple of stools, off to the side of the register, beside a box of magazines and a stack of napkins. The end of it was practically touching a dessert box, making it a potentially awkward place to tuck into fish and chips. But the tattooed man was so welcoming, and outside, the sky was threatening to rain. "I'll take it," I said.

He came out from behind the counter, asked my name, and ushered me to the high-top. I was seated at the edge of the open kitchen, with a view of the front door and the street, which turned out to be a terrific spot for people watching. Not unlike sitting at a bar.

What makes a table for one feel good? I've eaten alone in

other big cities, including Tokyo, where at the Moomin Bakery & Cafe in Tokyo Dome City solo diners are offered company in the form of large plush trolls known as Moomins (characters in the books by Tove Jansson). For a while, a Hello Kitty character called Keroppi also had its own theme café, where a solo diner could sit across from a frog. The tattooed man placed silverware and a carafe of water on my high-top, explaining, "In case you are thirsty." The more I dined alone in Paris, the more it seemed that I was treated not only well, but sometimes better than when I was accompanied. When my order was ready, he returned, all but singing my name as he sailed over with a golden fillet in a cardboard boat. "Fish and chips," he announced, lowering the plate. The fillet was nestled on a bed of crisp, browned fries and what appeared to be some sort of green tartar sauce, but was in fact a sublime-tasting (if not looking) green pea hash, so good I used it in lieu of ketchup. I picked up a fry as the rain began and the dry, gray stones on rue du Nil became wet and silver. The staff carried in the stools from the sidewalk and closed the tall windows, cocooning us inside. I had the right meal for a rainy afternoon: warm, crispy, a touch spicy, extremely comforting. The rain didn't last. Neither did the fries.

I was equally well looked after at the Minipalais, the hidden-in-plain-sight restaurant, bar, and lounge serving tasty modern French fare in the Grand Palais, off Cours la Reine, one of the few escapes from the throngs of tourists in the 8th arrondissement. One day I asked for a table on the terrace with the colonnades and potted palm trees, rattan armchairs, and mosaic floor overlooking Avenue Winston Churchill. The place was busy, yet the hostess offered several table options and was determined to find a menu in English, even though I told her not to bother, that I could make out enough of the French.

On another afternoon, on Boulevard du Montparnasse, I came upon La Closerie de Lilas, the restaurant and bar that's been around since the 1840s. It's been visited by the likes of Rimbaud, Fitzgerald, and Hemingway, who mentions it at least a half dozen times in *The Sun Also Rises* (much of which he wrote while at La Closerie). For years, a friend who grew up in France had been encouraging me to go, and more than once I had walked past its leafy terrace. This time, I went in.

It was humid, and I was flagging, carrying a couple of damp shopping bags. I had shown up at 3:30 in the afternoon, when business was all but dead and some sort of Muzak version of Kool & the Gang's "Joanna" was playing. As I followed a waiter into the brasserie, it didn't occur to me to ask to sit under the arbors instead.

There were only three occupied tables inside, and the zinc piano bar was empty, its shelves of liquor twinkling in the half-light. In a few hours it would be a bustling hive of well-heeled patrons drinking 18.50 euros "Pimm's Champagne" in the warm glow of red sconces. I put my assortment of damp bags on the chair across from me, embarrassed by them and by myself, and slid onto a maroon banquette. The Roman shades were down, making the place feel glum despite the glass ceiling as I draped a napkin across my lap. It seemed too late to get up and leave.

When the waiter returned, I ordered six large oysters. He scribbled in his notepad, then stopped, pen poised in midair, waiting.

I cocked my head and sat up straighter. He remained bent over the notepad, pen at the ready.

"And for after?" he asked, raising only his eyes.

I didn't want any "after." But rather than say so, I ordered more. I was sloppy and damp and didn't want to appear tight, on top of it all, which is how, on a spring day in Montparnasse, I came to eat an entire platter of oysters—and a plate of salmon and avocado tartare.

The tartare was good but the oysters—cool, wet, tasting faintly of the lemon I drizzled over them on their icy metal stand—were perfection. They were also nearly 30 euros. I suppose you could say, What price love? Or, as Eleanor Clark put it: "Obviously, if you don't love life, you can't enjoy an oyster."

Not long after *l'affaire* La Closerie, I took myself out for a less solemn meal on the Champs-Élysées. Number 140 is a two-story restaurant, with views over the wide sidewalk. People come and go toward the Arc de Triomphe and the traffic that curls around it. I opened the door, eased through the crowd toward the counter, and ordered a Filet-O-Fish sandwich.

And for after?

A vanilla hot fudge sundae. Total for dinner at McDonald's on the Champs-Élysées: 7.10 euros. I looked down at the Filet-O-Fish box. "*Savourez,*" it said. "Savor."

And I did.

# BEAUTY

# Musée de la Vie Romantique

*How to Be Alone in a Museum*

*Thanks to art, instead of seeing only one world, our own, we
see it under multiple forms, and as many as there are original
artists, just so many worlds have we at our disposal . . .*
—Marcel Proust, *In Search of Lost Time*

A t the end of the cobblestone path, the courtyard was
in bloom.

Tentacles of ivy reached out from the walls. Rose vines were
tangled above a bench. Lace cap hydrangea and hollyhocks
burst from their pots, and tiny white wildflowers gathered
around stray planters and filled the gaps between the steps. In
the middle of it all was an 1830s powder-pink mansion with
green shutters: the Musée de la Vie Romantique.

Piano music wafted from the drawing room, through the
entryway, out the stained-glass doors, and to the stairs beside
the tea garden, like a hostess saying softly, *Come in, come in.*

Inside, heavy drapes flanked the windows of the drawing
room, which had a floral rug and a dark portrait of George

Sand. On either side of a mantelpiece, the glow of electric candelabras was reflected in a large mirror. And in the middle of the room, four upholstered chairs circled a Louis XV desk and an unlit candelabra, as if at any moment a medium might arrive with a match and commence a séance to conjure the writer's ghost.

Though a "George Sand" family tree (showing both her pseudonym and her given name, Dupin) is displayed on a wall near the entryway, Sand herself never lived here. The museum is the former residence of the Dutch painter Ary Scheffer and now houses works and memorabilia of his and his better-known friends, including Sand, who on Fridays were invited to visit his studio.

The mansion is in New Athens, named for the district's neoclassical houses, on an ancient street called rue Chaptal, once home to a young Serge Gainsbourg, and the offices of Hot Club de France, "the jazz Parthenon of Paris," as Michael Dregni described it in *Django,* where Django Reinhardt and Duke Ellington played.

In a room off the entrance of the museum are also keepsakes that belonged to Sand, including a plaster cast of her lover's left hand by Auguste Clésinger. The lover was Chopin, who also walked these halls, as did Rossini, Liszt, and Delacroix, himself a proponent of alone time. (His former apartment and studio on the beautiful Place de Furstenberg is a museum as well.) "How can one keep one's enthusiasm concentrated on a subject when one is always at the mercy of other people and in constant need of their society?" he wondered in his journal. "The things we experience for ourselves when we are alone are much stronger and much fresher."

Research suggests this is true. One study, part of a project supported by the Swiss National Science Foundation, found that visitors who attended an exhibition at a fine-art museum with other people found it significantly less thought-provoking, were less convinced by the exhibition design, and were less able to enjoy the museum space in silence than those who toured the museum alone. Those who went with companions experienced the beauty of the artworks to a lesser extent, and were less able to experience a deep connection to the art.

For the study, more than five hundred and fifty visitors to the Kunstmuseum St. Gallen in Switzerland were given an electronic data glove to wear as they toured the museum. The glove enabled the researchers to record the paths of the participants, as well as other information, including the time they spent in front of the artworks, their speed, heart rate, and fluctuations in skin conductance level, a potential indicator of emotional processes. The subjects also filled out visitor surveys before entering the exhibition and after leaving it.

The study, published in the journal *Museum Management and Curatorship*, found that conversation interfered with visitors' making a connection to the art. People who weren't discussing the art with a companion were more frequently and more strongly emotionally stimulated by it. They were able to "enter the exhibition with 'all of their senses open and alert' to a greater degree."

When I go to a museum with friends, I remember the

outing. When I go alone, I remember the art. Certainly, visiting a museum as a social occasion is a wonderful way to spend time with people we love. But there are also upsides to going by oneself, as the research suggests. A person's response to a work of art may be an emotional, private experience. There are paintings and sculptures you want to fall into, wrestle with, or simply sit across from in silence.

Indeed, while conventional wisdom holds that social interaction helps museum visitors learn by discussing what they're seeing with fellow attendees, a study published in *Curator: The Museum Journal*, challenged that notion, showing that there is no meaningful learning advantage to going with others or going alone; both can be equally beneficial, just in different ways. In the weeks after their visit, "solitary visitors were just as likely as paired visitors to have discussed the things they had seen or learned with family or friends," researchers at Queensland University of Technology in Brisbane, Australia, reported. For the study some forty solo visitors and forty visitors in pairs were observed and interviewed during their visit to the Queensland Museum. Four weeks later, 40 percent of participants took part in a follow-up telephone interview. When asked how being on their own contributed to their experience, the most common response was that it allowed them to explore the exhibition at their own pace. Other reasons offered related to having greater choice and control, and freedom from distraction. Participants had responses like "I can look at what I want to look at," "I can get more immersed in it," "I can feel what I feel without input from others," and "You miss more when you are in a group."

Alone, we can also personalize our visit. Sandra Jackson-

Dumont, who oversees the education programs at the Metropolitan Museum of Art in New York, once suggested that museumgoers "curate" their own experience by researching the collection ahead of time and choosing particular subjects or themes (gardens, oceans, dogs) of personal interest. A museum's information desk can provide guidance, and larger institutions often offer online itineraries for thematic or abbreviated tours. One at the Louvre, for example, winds past a dozen masterpieces—including the Venus de Milo, the *Mona Lisa,* and the Great Sphinx of Tanis—in an hour and a half. The free questions and lesson plans that museums like the Metropolitan Museum of Art and the Vatican Museums in Rome post online for students are valuable for adults, too. To further personalize the experience, Jackson-Dumont said we may also want to make our own music playlist at home and take headphones to the museum, letting us walk the galleries with Drake or Debussy.

Sometimes, we want the walk to be leisurely so we can read every last bit of wall text, or enjoy an audio tour in its entirety. Other times, we want to move at a clip. For instance, on a spring day in Paris I didn't want to spend the sunniest hours inside the dim Musée Nissim de Camondo with its French furniture from the eighteenth century. At an exhibition called *La Toilette: The Invention of Privacy* at the Musée Marmottan Monet, I didn't stay long because the galleries were packed. The show explored how, over centuries, the toilette went from being a social space, where women were accompanied by chambermaids and family, to one of solitude, even contemplation. There were paintings from the Degas series After the Bath and Pierre Bonnard's *Marthe à la toilette* (1919), in which Marthe "seems to be thinking, allowing herself long moments alone," as the wall text suggested. I was interested in the show, but moved swiftly; looking at a painting is different when we have the physical space to forget where we are than when strangers are accidentally brushing our shoulder or moving into our line of vision.

On the other hand, at a different time, while viewing the work of the contemporary Brazilian artist Vik Muniz at the Maison Européenne de la Photographie in the Marais, I was delighted to linger. The show included his *After the Bath, After Degas (Pictures of Magazine 2)*, 2011, an interpretation of the series by Degas, in which the image of the solitary nude woman is composed of ripped magazine pages and paper with parts of women's faces and bodies on them. Muniz does with food, dirt, and junk what the Impressionists and Pointillists did with paint. He used melted chocolate to create a snapshot of faces in a crowd in *Individuals (From Pictures of Chocolate)*, 1998, and pasta sauce to play off of Caravaggio's *Testa di Medusa*, rechristening it *Medusa Marinara*, 1999. The museum was practically empty the morning I arrived. It was the first time I'd seen Muniz's work, and I was able to experience the joy of discovery, unselfconsciously. I could get up close to *After the Bath* to examine the colors and shapes of the individual magazine fragments, then back away to appreciate how they formed the whole.

Yet the museum experience isn't always about the particular works on view. A museum itself can be a "restorative environment," a place that may "create a sense of peace and calm that permits people to recover their cognitive and emotional effectiveness," as Stephen Kaplan, an evolutionary psychologist at the University of Michigan, and colleagues explained in the journal *Environment and Behavior.*

For me, this has almost always been true. Like a church or temple, a museum has its own physical and psychic architecture. Abstract art or dinosaur bones may anchor us to the world, while the space itself allows the mind to drift, free-associating, making meaning. This tranquility can be felt as much in the blank white box of a modern art museum just as it can in the dark, galactic halls of a planetarium. It can be experienced in sculpture halls amid frozen white nudes, or in a flowering courtyard between galleries.

I was a teenager when the first major retrospective in the United States in twenty-five years of René Magritte's work opened at the Metropolitan Museum of Art. During a class trip, we were allowed to split up and wander on our own among paintings of jingle bells and green apples. It was my introduction to Magritte, and I was taken with the bowler hats, the floating baguettes, the French words, and black umbrellas, at once playful and unsettling. I stood in front of the paintings, charged by the pleasure of discovery, not necessarily of something in them, but in me.

Alone, we can form a special relationship with art, observed Stéphane Debenedetti in the *International Journal of Arts Management.* Further, the "elevated, austere, even magical atmosphere of a museum," as he described it, may allow for "self-reflection, tranquillity and personal freedom." It may enable visitors "to develop identity and self-knowledge free of social constraints." In other words, museums can help foster self-actualization.

Yet despite the potential benefits of a solo museum visit,

many people are likely to forgo the experience, according to a series of studies by Rebecca K. Ratner, a professor of marketing at the Robert H. Smith School of Business at the University of Maryland, and Rebecca W. Hamilton, a professor of marketing at the McDonough School of Business at Georgetown University.

Participants in one study predicted that going to a movie or an art exhibition wouldn't be as much fun if they went alone, and they worried that people might infer that they didn't have many friends. Yet when the participants actually explored an art gallery by themselves, their enjoyment of the experience did not significantly differ from that of the people who attended in pairs. By our not being willing to go alone, the researchers wrote in the *Journal of Consumer Research,* we miss out on opportunities—experiences that can be pleasurable, intellectually stimulating, and lead to new, possibly meaningful connections with strangers (more on that later).

In the same way that arriving at a museum with a companion doesn't mean we have to tour the galleries with them, going alone doesn't have to be completely isolating, either. We can break up periods of solitude by chatting with a docent or attending a lecture. Many museums today make it easy to be on our own yet still feel a sense of connection through guided tours, talks, and apps with audio tours. (Smartphone walking tours of cities like London and Tokyo, as well as places throughout the United States, are yet another resource; check out the Tips and Tools guide at the end of this book.)

The novelist John Steinbeck once wrote about how overwhelming it could feel when visiting a vast museum like the

Uffizi or the Prado. But later, after he had time alone to think about all that he had seen, he could return to the galleries to revisit those particular works that had spoken to him.

"After confusion I can go into the Prado in Madrid and pass unseeing the thousand pictures shouting for my attention," he wrote in *Travels with Charley*, about his solo (if you don't count his French poodle) road trip across America, "and I can visit a friend."

———

Outside the Musée de la Vie Romantique, in the shade of tree boughs and umbrellas, visitors were spread across benches and café chairs in the tea garden with pink roses. I crossed the courtyard to the shady path between the high latticed walls back to the sidewalk.

In a way, all of Paris is a museum of romantic life. For centuries its apartments, churches, bars, and restaurants have provided reprieves for men and women who prized their alone time. Because of that, it's easy to conclude that there must be hundreds of artists' and writers' homes in the city that are regularly open to the public. But there are, in fact, few of the latter, like the Maison de Victor Hugo in the 4th arrondissement in Place des Vosges, and the Maison de Balzac in the 16th arrondissement. What typically remains of writers are museums that feature re-creations of their workspaces, resurrected using the personal objects that outlived them, as is the case for Marcel Proust.

One morning in the Marais, I heard in the distance the belch of a tuba playing a sleepy, old-fashioned refrain. It was merry, though not exuberant; a fragile kind of joy. It sounded like the backdrop to a gathering and indeed, when I turned the corner from Square Georges-Cain I found that a small crowd had formed on rue des Francs-Bourgeois.

The tuba was in the arms of a salty-haired man in shorts and sandals. Beside him were a clarinet player, a banjo player, and an older woman in an overcoat and an olive beret with a flower on the side, dancing in place like a marionette, snapping her fingers, kicking her feet in moves from another time.

Across the street, behind huge wrought-iron gates, was the central garden of the Musée Carnavalet, two townhouses that chronicle the history of Paris, from prehistoric canoes to recreations of centuries-old rooms with objects that once belonged to notable Parisians, like Proust's brass bed from which he wrote much of *In Search of Lost Time*. The *tutt-tutt* of the tuba trailed after me as I passed under the archway, past the low hedge mazes with colorful flowers poking up, inside to the ticket counter. Admission, said the man behind the desk, was free, because the museum was preparing for a renovation. I remarked on my luck. He made a face and explained that regrettably many rooms were already closed, though I wasn't discouraged. There are about a hundred rooms in the Carnavalet and on that particular day, I was there for only one.

We chatted for a short while about this and that, and where I was from, before I waved goodbye and walked through a courtyard and into galleries with elaborate metal signs, some as old as the sixteenth century. There were signs shaped like giant scissors for a tailor, a fork for an innkeeper, a key for a locksmith, so that even customers who couldn't read would know what the various shopkeepers offered. A painted sheet metal "Chat Noir" sign shaped like a shabby, yellow-eyed cat with its tail curled around a crescent moon was hanging from the ceiling. In the late 1800s, it hung outside the Chat Noir cabaret in Montmartre.

I walked upstairs through room after room of ornate furniture, past Madame de Sévigné's desk (she lived in the Carnavalet for nearly twenty years), thinking with each step that the next room would be Proust's. He had lined it with cork to keep out noise, which made the belching tuba out front particularly droll.

I arrived at the end of a long hall and then retraced my steps, but there was nowhere else to go. I reached into my back pocket, unfolded the museum brochure with shaded rooms indicating which areas were closed, and discovered that they included room 147—the one with furniture from apartments where Proust used to live.

And so, in the end, I saw the brass bed from which Proust wrote *In Search of Lost Time* not in room 147 of the Musée Carnavalet but on a postcard in the gift shop. It was a bit dreary. The brass bed was pushed up against yellow, cork-lined walls, giving the setup an institutional air. The actual apartment where the bed and cork walls had been was about two and a half miles away, and it had become a bank.

To conjure Proust in Paris, it's more fun to do so in one of his old haunts. There are many, including the sprawling Bois de Boulogne on the west end of the city. But as Proust himself appreciated quietude—"I discover pleasures of another kind," he wrote in *In Search of Lost Time*, "of tasting the good scent on the air, of not being disturbed by any visitor"—I decided to go someplace more intimate: Parc Monceau.

———

The long streets of pale stone houses, immaculate and symmetrical with their tall windows and wrought iron balconies, were practically blinding in the sun. It was unseasonably hot, more like walking the old city in Istanbul than the 8th arrondissement.

In the nineteenth century, this area went from being a commune on the outskirts of the city to its latest wealthy neighborhood. It attracted banking families like the Rothschilds; the Méniers, the French chocolatiers (who eventually sold their business to Nestlé); Henri Cernuschi, a leader of the Lombard revolution of 1848 and an Asian art collector; and yet another prominent banking dynasty, the Camondos, who once owned one of the largest banks in the Ottoman Empire. The family's former mansion at 63 rue de Monceau is now a museum, named for the son of Count Moise de Camondo, who was born in Istanbul and became a Parisian banker and art collector.

Smaller, less-frequented museums, particularly those that were once homes, feel made for solitary visitors. Their intimacy seems to say, *This painting, this sculpture, exist only for you.* The Musée Nissim de Camondo is not modest—it was modeled after Louis XV's Petit Trianon, the Greek-inspired château amid the gardens at Versailles—though it feels personal nevertheless. It's been widely praised for its extraordinary collection of eighteenth-century furniture and objets d'art—a mahogany rolltop desk by Claude-Charles Saunier is said to be one of the highlights—but I confess I was more interested in the bones of the house and the flowering park beside it than in the desk.

I wound through rooms: the great study, the great drawing room, the dining room, the small study, the porcelain room where the count dined when he was alone. The wood paneling was dark, the carpet thick, the drapes and velvet chairs of another time, another season. From a high window I looked down to see a handful of people sketching on folding chairs and stools on the grass and pebbled paths in the family's private garden beside Parc Monceau.

Monet made half a dozen landscape paintings of the park in 1876 and in 1878. In one, women in white frocks and hats sit in the shade at a bend in a leafy path, children at their feet. Another—a swirl of green, pink, and yellow—captures the fertility of the park in springtime, just as it was on this particular afternoon.

There's an entrance to the park around the corner from the Camondo house. Tall black and gilt gates lead to a short block where, at the end, another set of gates, far less grand, ring the park, inaugurated by Napoleon III in 1861. A photograph of Proust in Parc Monceau as a teenager shows him standing beside his friend Antoinette Faure at her birthday party. (Her father, Félix Faure, would one day become the president of France.) It was Antoinette who asked Proust to complete what was known as a confession album, "An Album to Record Thoughts, Feelings, etc.," which eventually evolved into various versions of the Proust Questionnaire, including *Vanity Fair*'s regular feature that begins by asking, "What is your idea of perfect happiness?"

Monceau provided both a respite and fodder for artists and writers. Zola described it in *Nana* as the "luxurious quarter at that time springing up in the vague district which had once been the Plaine Monceau." Henry James called it "one of the prettiest corners of Paris." Colette said the park's "soft lawns veiled in misty curtains of spray from the sprinklers" attracted her "like something good to eat." She also liked that Monceau had fewer children than the Luxembourg Gardens, declaring, "It was better altogether."

The Prousts lived at 45 rue de Courcelles, a five-minute walk from the Camondo mansion. Flaubert lived between them at 4 rue Murillo, Parc Monceau. I wound around the paths they walked, the paths their characters walked. People and roses were withering in the heat. Schoolchildren in sandals and baseball caps circled an Egyptian pyramid. A barefoot woman filled a yellow pail at a fountain. A boy, not quite up to his father's waist, strolled beside him in the shade. This is what Monet's paintings capture: the conviviality of park life, the gathering of families.

The springtime paintings of a lesser-known Impressionist, Gustave Caillebotte, however, depict "a more solitary vision of the park," as a Sotheby's auction catalogue once put it. In one painting, a gentleman in a suit and hat walks alone along a leafy, curving path. I followed one just like it.

Every now and then along the oblong perimeter of Monceau dotted with weathered green benches, paths slice in, leading past sculptures—here, a composer; there, a playwright—on grounds dense with unruly ferns and shrubs. There are beds of slender wildflowers, a carousel, a pond, and follies like a Venetian-inspired bridge and the pyramid, closer to the size of a teepee than anything you'll find at Giza. There's even a Renaissance archway that was once part of the former Paris City Hall. Yet what caught my eye were the plaques amid the leaves along a fence. They depicted a man alone in the basket of a hot air balloon, a nod to the world's first frameless parachute jump in 1797 by the balloonist André-Jacques Garnerin, thousands of feet above the ground on which I was standing.

Garnerin's wife, Jeanne-Geneviève, was the first woman to jump from a parachute. And his niece, Elisa Garnerin, made more than three dozen professional parachute descents between 1815 and 1836, according to the *Telegraph* in London. (Before her, the balloonist Marie Madeleine-Sophie Blanchard made more than sixty-five solo ascents, until an 1819 attempt proved fatal.)

Women frequently flew alone. That may have been because a companion is not technically necessary, as S.L. Kotar and J.E. Gessler write in *Ballooning: A History, 1782–1900*, or because the women wanted to make sure that any fame they garnered wouldn't be attributed to a man flying with them.

But perhaps they did so simply because they enjoyed flying solo. After all, it wasn't uncommon for early women explorers to have a taste for solitude. Take Marianne North, the Englishwoman who in the 1800s circumnavigated the globe unaccompanied, spending thirteen years traveling and skirting Victorian convention. Her paintings of flowers and landscapes hang at the Royal Botanic Gardens at Kew, outside central London.

In her autobiography she recounts her travels, which she didn't begin until she was forty. In Nainital in the Himalayas in India's Uttarakhand state, she liked sitting in the sun. In Philadelphia, she walked the parks and Zoological Gardens enjoying idle days. In the Bunya Mountains of Queensland, Australia, she said she enjoyed "my entire solitude through the grand forest alone." Today, a genus of tree and several plant species are named for her.

The spring afternoon felt like summer. People were painting, sketching, lolling in the grass, eating their lunches on benches. I made my way along a shady path edged with pink blooms, like Caillebotte's man in the hat, sunlight flickering as I passed under a tree bough.

# Window-Licking

*Finding Your Muse*

"*Errer est humain, flâner est parisien*": "*To wander is human, to stroll is Parisian.*"

—Victor Hugo, *Les Misérables*

South Pigalle, the neighborhood at the base of Montmartre, was once the "center of the flesh-and-feather shows," as the *New York Times* described it in the 1960s. Today, it's SoPi, the center of hipster brunches, quartier of man-buns, vintage guitars, and shops with names like Funky Junk and Finger in the Nose.

I spent a morning there at Buvette on rue Henry Monnier, eating *brouillés saumon:* scrambled eggs with salmon and bread, topped with a dollop of crème fraiche and two fat, lightly salty capers. Jazz lilted in the background and sunlight streamed through the open door, bouncing off the decorative tin ceiling tiles, not quite reaching back to the spot at the marble bar where I was sitting on an old-fashioned Toledo-style drafting stool.

On the bar were wire baskets of limes and lemons; little carafes of orange and grapefruit juice; striped straws and mason jars of black olives; bottles of wine piled like kindling in a shallow silver bowl. How French—or so it seems. The Paris Buvette is an ex-pat in disguise, an offshoot of Buvette in New York's West Village.

I paid the bill and wandered across the street to a shop with a Photax camera in the window and a straw basket of used records on the sidewalk. A few doors down was Le Rocketship, a coffee and home design boutique. Looking in the windows felt like peering into an aquarium with tropical fish. There were Caran d'Ache pens in fluorescent pink and green; handmade ceramic mugs, each decorated with a single colorful dot; shocking yellow Japanese Washi paper masking tape. The previous day, in Le Bon Marché, I had admired bright white pencils in a canister, arranged like stems in a vase. What is it about office supplies that's so irresistible? They seem to hold the promise of new beginnings.

In no hurry and accountable to no one, I went into Le Rocketship and examined Grand Voyageur leather journals, handmade copper lamps that looked like rockets, bright boxes of paper clips shaped like airplanes and motorcycles, a red metal platter that read "Come with me 2 Zanzibar." Everything seemed to whisper, *Let's run away*. It was the sort of shop where you want it all and yet, you suspect that possessing any one object would be unsatisfying. The joy was not in the owning, but in the looking; in seeing the sundries there, flocked together, like a pretty crowd at a garden party.

And so I left them and went on my way, past Place Gustave

Toudouze, a little leafy square crowded with tables and umbrellas for a tea shop, pizza joint, and Indian restaurant. At
L'Oeuf there were shark puppets, bohemian bracelets, and rub-
ber chickens. Handbags, some shaped like teddy bear heads,
were displayed, if one could call it that, in a back room around
the perimeter of the floor, the way a child might set up a pre-
tend boutique in her bedroom. I stopped at the windows of
Jamini, the Franco-Indian lifestyle brand, where patterned pil-
lows and rugs with zigzags and peacock eyespots peeked out
from painted metal trunks.

In the United States, we call this pleasurable wandering
along storefronts window-shopping. In France, the pastime—
*faire du lèche-vitrines*—translates to a more passionate name:
"window-licking," which seems to prioritize admiration over
consumption.

For centuries the city's shopkeepers have labored to catch
the eye of the passerby. By the nineteenth century, Parisians
were accustomed to walking the boulevards and streets to
"ever-changing panoramas; continual exhibitions of masterpieces; worlds of sorrows, universes of joy," as Balzac wrote.
They passed elegant shop signs and strolled Paris's arcades—
covered passages, of which there were once more than one
hundred. A handful from the nineteenth century still remain—
like Galerie Vivienne, Passage Choiseul, Passage Jouffroy, and
Passage Verdeau—featuring lanterns, sun umbrellas, and potted trees, as if their sleepy postcard and antique shops were outdoors and not beneath vaulted glass ceilings.

In an artfully arranged shop, in the right frame of mind,
browsing alone doesn't feel transactional but more like

wandering an art gallery. In some places, the shop *is* also a gallery, like 0fr, the bookshop, publisher, and gallery where a visitor can stock up on graphic art, photography, and music and fashion magazines. This is shopping as experience, not necessarily for acquisition. Alone, we can develop our aesthetic sense at our own pace, be it for late medieval bedroom furniture at the Musée des Arts Décoratifs, or the "bazar chic" style (espadrilles, striped bohemian daybed cushions) of the French model Inès de la Fressange at her boutique in the 7th arrondissement.

We can let ourselves drift toward the windows of a shop with piles of stamps from Bhutan and Vietnam, or to those of Librairie Maritime Outremer, where artifacts like a compass and sundial are scattered among books about travel. Exploring art, fashion, design, and plant shops—ceramic tableware at Astier de Villatte, spools of ribbonry and braid at Petit Pan Paris—might inspire a creative endeavor, decor for your living room, even how you want to spend the rest of your life. The supplies at Le Rocketship got me thinking not only about how I wanted my workspace to look, but also about what I wanted to accomplish there, while the vase of stark white pencils at Le Bon Marché simply instructed: "Begin!"

The writer and actress Lena Dunham of *Girls* (who used to describe herself in her Twitter bio as a "hermit about town") has said that time alone helped her discover what it was she loved doing. "I spent a whole semester in college just knitting and watching old VHS tapes, and I consider it one of the happiest times in my life because I had a chance to connect to my passions and who I really am," she told *InStyle* magazine.

It's not surprising that Dunham found it to be one of the

most gratifying periods in her life. Peak happiness experiences tend to be those that are "tightly linked to your sense of who you are or want to be," as the professors and psychologists Elizabeth Dunn, of the University of British Columbia in Vancouver, and Michael Norton, of Harvard Business School, wrote. So it's worth spending some time discovering what gets us excited, what gets us going.

Whatever our interest—playing the violin, tending a garden—it can, as Anthony Storr explained, be a significant part of what gives life meaning. "Even those who have the happiest relationships," he said, "need something other than those relationships to complete their fulfillment."

Pursuing our natural passions is known as "intrinsic motivation," or "doing something because it is inherently interesting or enjoyable," as opposed to external motivations, like work evaluations or other people's opinions, as Richard M. Ryan and Edward L. Deci, psychology professors at the University of Rochester in New York, have described it. In our healthiest states, we are "active, inquisitive, curious, and playful creatures, displaying a ubiquitous readiness to learn and explore," they wrote in *Contemporary Educational Psychology*, a journal.

To explore, we need only put one foot in front of the other.

In fact, walking can significantly boost creative thinking. While we might certainly encounter stimulating things along the way, researchers at Stanford University found that it's the very act of walking, even indoors on a treadmill facing a blank wall, that helps new ideas flow. Participants in the Stanford study were encouraged to talk aloud to a researcher while walking, so it's unclear if the results would be the same for solitary strolls, though anecdotally there are countless examples of thinkers, artists, and everyday Joes and Janes having their creativity sparked by perambulating.

In Paris I walked everywhere. Well, almost. Some places require a key, like Avenue Frochot in the 9th arrondissement, where behind the gate with the blue sign that warns *Voie Privée* (Private Way) are the former homes and workshops of artists and writers, from the creator of *The Three Musketeers*, Alexandre Dumas, to Jean-Paul Gaultier, the creator of the cone bras Madonna wore during her "Blond Ambition" tour in the 1990s, as well as Victor Hugo (who stayed there with his friend, the writer Paul Meurice), Toulouse-Lautrec, Renoir, and Moreau. Walk around to Place Pigalle and you can see that the street dead-ends at a graffitied, corrugated wall between a Monop' (a smaller Monoprix) and a pharmacy. A passerby wouldn't have the faintest idea of what was on the other side. Only the striped cat asleep in the middle of the street knows.

Happily, there are more roads accessible to strollers than not. I walked through Canal Saint-Martin, where I went to buy Bensimon sneakers (the French cousins of Keds and, in my opinion, more comfortable), and browse the coffee table books at Artazart. Garbage and empty bottles floated like ducks in the canal's pea-soup water. But in the right light—when a ray of sun shot between the trees that lined the water, backlighting lovers on a footbridge—it had all the romance of a Monet bridge over water lilies.

"People who open themselves to the beauty and excellence around them are more likely to find joy, meaning, and profound connections in their lives," wrote Sonja Lyubomirsky of the University of California, Riverside.

Paris makes this easy. It's attractive, charming, historic, and walkable—qualities that research by the Project for Public Spaces, a nonprofit organization, found contribute to making an ideal shared space. I walked the medieval streets of the Marais, the Bois de Boulogne, the cobblestone hills of Montmartre. I passed petanque courts and apartments with striped awnings, stopping to browse French creams in a Monoprix or stand in a boulangerie line—one time catching a waiter dash in and reemerge, his tray piled with croissants as if in some period farce.

"Oh! to stroll about Paris! What an adorable and delightful existence!," wrote Balzac. "To walk is to vegetate; to stroll is to live."

I chose to live.

———

About an hour and a half west on foot, in the 16th arrondissement, the sidewalks climb high above the city. You don't necessarily realize just how high until you pass a staircase that falls off into nowhere, or look down from the traffic circle at Place du Costa Rica to the nest of train tracks around Pont Bir Hakeim.

On weekdays, it's quieter in this wealthy residential neighborhood than in other central areas. You can find yourself walking alone for vast stretches between Haussmannian mansions, lost in thought. Had I not glanced to my left as I was passing Avenue de Camoens, a sleepy, dead-end street where ivy drips from the balconies of stone mansions, I would have walked right past an unobstructed view of the Eiffel Tower.

It was a fortuitous sighting. There were no onlookers with smartphones at the ready. There was no one at all. I crossed the boulevard and walked toward a streetlamp on a stone balustrade at the end of the street where flights of stairs, some green with algae, plunged down. I looked over the trees and the gray and silver rooftops, far from the crowds at Champ de Mars.

When I eventually returned to the sidewalk, I turned onto a quiet, sloping road whose limestone mansions seemed as if they would go on forever, though every now and then there was a chance to break away—a place where a balustrade disappeared and in its place was a staircase down to who knows where. Some stairways are wide. Others, like rue des Eaux, are narrow alleys between buildings, shaded and mossy at the edges. I was on rue Raynouard in Passy, formerly the outskirts of Paris, where Benjamin Franklin lived during his ambassadorship to France, and trees and streetlamps accompany a pedestrian along the way.

At one point the sidewalk jagged, and there was neither staircase nor mansion—just a freestanding stone archway with wide, teal French doors, like an image from some Surrealist painting. One of the doors was closed, while the other had a large knocker. Beyond it lay a steep flight of stairs. I went through the open door, under the decorative wrought-iron transom, and took a step down.

Holding the paint-chipped railing I descended lower and lower until I was far beneath the level of the street, on the other side of a vast wall. There, on a little cobblestone patio, stood a house unlike any other I'd encountered. It was a pale, low-slung cottage, with teal shutters that matched the double doors at the top of the hill: number 47 rue Raynouard—Balzac's doorstep.

He lived in an apartment in that house for about seven years, beginning in 1840, where it was not uncommon for him to work up to sixteen hours a day, writing and rewriting, including books in his series *The Human Comedy*. The house, now a museum, is just right for wandering alone. The stairs are narrow, and the wood floors creak. Visitors there are quiet and slow and often on their own. On display are books from Balzac's personal library, proofs with his corrections, his work table and armchair, Rodin's studies for a sculpture of the writer's head, and Balzac's 1834 walking stick "bubbling with turquoise," as he described it, on a gold knob with thin tassels—a cane that he said had more success than all his works.

On the walls are original editions, manuscripts, and half-man, half-beast lithographs by the French artist and sometime Balzac collaborator J.J. Grandville: elephant men, bird people, a dog with the head of a man, a snake in women's finery. The caricatures almost demanded a kind of intimacy of engagement, to be viewed one at a time, one person at a time.

Outside, below the thick ivy overtaking the latticework on the high wall to the street, is a small garden with assorted green metal chairs and benches amid the roses, overlooking the Eiffel Tower. Relaxed and nonchalant, it lacks the size, symmetry, and manicured perfection of the city's formal gardens which, you don't necessarily realize until you're standing in its grass, comes as a relief. I thought of my friends' happy backyard garden at the house by the bay.

Along a narrow dirt path around the bushes, a man on a garden chair was engrossed in a book. Beyond him, toward the back of the house, past the roses with soft petals beginning to brown and curl at the edges, were a pair of crumbling sphinxes. Their front paws were broken; their noses, too.

At one point after Balzac's death, Marquet de Vasselot, a member of the Société des Gens de Lettres, a writer's group that was commissioning a statue of Balzac, proposed that a sculpture be made portraying him as a winged sphinx. Ultimately, the public monument was entrusted to Rodin who, somewhat controversially, depicted Balzac in the dressing gown (it has subsequently been likened to a bathrobe) he wore around the house while writing and drinking copious amounts of coffee.

The sphinxes in the garden had lion's bodies and human heads and were crouching on either side of the path beside the house. You can make a game of finding sphinxes around Paris: outside the Hôtel de Sully, in the courtyard of the Musée du Louvre's Gallerie des Antiques, around a fountain at Place du Châtelet, on the quai Aimé-Césaire along the Jardin des Tuileries.

Beyond the Eiffel Tower, it looked like rain. I sat on an empty bench. There was no waiting for better weather. There's no waiting for ideal circumstances to enjoy the garden, to count sphinxes, to be open to wonder.

"The time to savor," Bryant said, "is now."

## PART II

Summer

# Istanbul

# NERVE

# Üsküdar

*The Art of Anticipation*

> *The more I surrendered to myself, to the self that would not
> be limited and narrowly defined, the more glorious a time I
> had with me and with life. I stayed open, ready, breathless
> even, for adventure.*
>
> —Eartha Kitt, *Rejuvenate! (It's Never Too Late)*

Our little ferry looked like a life raft compared to the colossal tankers it was skirting on the Bosporus, the storied strait that slices between the hills of Europe and Asia. None of the passengers seemed concerned. People dangled their legs off the back of the boat and leaned over the bars along the sides, turning their faces to the hot breeze, the white sailboats, and the blue water sparkling in the sun. August in Istanbul.

Men circled the wood benches of riders, carrying trays of tea and neatly arranged snacks, trying to drum up customers as we moved farther from the European shore and the high walls of the Ciragan Palace Kempinski, the sumptuous hotel where I had recently checked in. There, beyond the palm and pink blooming Erguvan trees, in guest rooms with beds with tasseled canopies, it was easy to slip into an Ottoman-era fantasy.

Ciragan, just east of the seaside Dolmabahçe Palace, began as a sixteenth-century mansion and takes its name from the Farsi word for "light." It's been the home of sultans and their harems; was built, demolished, and rebuilt over the centuries with rare marble and mother of pearl; destroyed by fire and theft; and was reborn in the 1980s, when construction for the luxury hotel began.

Hundreds of years ago, it was renowned for feasts that were held in the area, and during my first stay in the city it was still hosting lavish parties. One night I would happen upon a wedding on the sprawling waterfront terrace; another night, an elaborate corporate celebration with belly dancers. Yet the festivities didn't take place only along the water. They happened *on* the water, too, on yachts glowing with colorful lights, no doubt gliding to and from the city's nightclubs. I would watch them from a quiet table at the hotel's summer restaurant along the Bosporus, which offered an enormous buffet—the sort a traveler begins fantasizing about long before dinnertime— with chafing dishes and platters of lamb, salmon, *manti* with sweet tomato sauce, roasted vegetables, beans, yogurt, and spicy oil. Turkish coffee was served with glistening baklava on a silver tray as the setting sun bathed the Asian coast of the city and the windows of the houses on the hillside in soft, pink light. Hanging lanterns and streetlamps with globes would begin to glow, and the staff would light candles along the garden paths. Ornate narghiles (hookahs) were brought to tables beneath the trees outside Le Fumoir Bar, perfuming the night air with the scent of sweet tobacco.

In the mornings, people would swim in the infinity pool beside the Bosporous and eat browned pastries from silver baskets at round tables on the patio. But on this particular morning, I was on a little ferry speeding away from it all and, in mere minutes, had made the journey from Europe to Asia.

We were on the shores of Üsküdar, an area of Istanbul once known as the City of Gold, where Ottoman-era mosques stand silhouetted against the sky and satellite dishes seem to be mounted outside every apartment window. The passengers wobbled off the lurching boat along a seawall protected by cracked tires as commuters boarded nearby ferries lined with orange life preservers. Boys sat at the foot of the water, watching ships and seagulls come and go.

Days before I arrived in Istanbul, the borough president of Brooklyn, New York, signed what's known as a sister city agreement. "Brooklyn is America's Üsküdar," he declared, probably to the great surprise of the residents of Brooklyn and Üsküdar.

Turkey's *Daily Sabah* pointed out that both cities have diverse populations with mosques, synagogues, and churches, and that, like Brooklyn, Üsküdar is "a place for hip and urban citizens with an artsy character." Hilmi Türkmen, the mayor of the Üsküdar municipality, likened the Bosporus Bridge (since renamed the July 15th Martyrs Bridge) to the Brooklyn Bridge. "Two sisters," he said, according to the *Sabah*, "have met through bridges of the soul."

While Americans may be surprised to learn of its status as a sister city, some may be familiar with Üsküdar through the Turkish folk song "Uska Dara," which became a hit for Eartha Kitt in the 1950s, one of several Turkish songs she learned while performing in Istanbul early in her career. "Üsküdar is a little town in Turkey," Kitt tells the listener in English, but it played a big role in history. The Sacred Caravan used its harbor to depart for Mecca and Medina "with its long train of pilgrims and its sacred white camel bearing gifts from the Sultan to the Serif of Mecca," as Hilary Sumner-Boyd and John Freely described it in *Strolling Through Istanbul*.

Such were the things I discovered in the weeks before leaving for the city. In advance of all of my trips I would dip into the culture by reading novels and poetry, watching films and television programs, and browsing fashion, travel, and design blogs. Doing this, relishing how enjoyable an upcoming experience might be, isn't just edifying—it can boost our spirits long before we even leave for the airport.

"Anticipation is a free form of happiness," Elizabeth Dunn found in her research on well-being, "the one that's least vulnerable to things going wrong." When I'm able, I book flights months in advance (for Istanbul it was six) and then commence daydreaming about all the things I might want to see, taste, and try. Hours are spent reading about local cuisine, art, and history. I sought classic guidebooks and travelogues like Edmondo De Amicis's *Constantinople*; novels by Tanpinar; poetry; and design books such as *Zeynep Fadillioğlu: Bosphorus and Beyond*, which showcases Fadillioğlu's work from glossy nightclubs like Ulus 29 to the Şakirin mosque in Üsküdar.

Dunn has not only studied anticipation, but can personally attest to its effectiveness. She once spent months planning and fantasizing about a trip to Hawaii, only to arrive in Oahu and be attacked by a ten-foot tiger shark. She was bitten to the bone—thankfully without suffering any physical impairments—but when she recounted the story she was quick to point out that even a shark attack couldn't take away the joy and excitement she experienced all those months in advance of the trip. It was, as she put it, happiness already in the bank.

The trick to doing this right is not to get wedded to an itinerary, as I did in Paris the night I left Les Éditeurs. Being too rigid puts you at risk for unfavorably comparing your expectations to the real thing. And it doesn't allow room for serendipity. A study in the *Journal of Experimental Social Psychology* in the 1990s found that people tended to view positive experiences—a vacation in Europe, a bicycle trip through California, a Thanksgiving getaway—as a little more positive both before and after they occurred than in realtime, a phenomenon Terence R. Mitchell and colleagues referred to as "rosy prospection" and "rosy retrospection."

To have the best trip possible when we're actually on it, we need to stay loose. "One of the arts of savoring experiences and vacation is to let go of all that expectation," Bryant explained. If you don't, you're never really allowing yourself to be in the moment, but are "always comparing it to what you thought it would be." The joy of the moment may also involve surprises, and those surprises may well turn out to be some of our favorite parts of a trip.

Of course, there are times when the issue isn't simply that

reality fails to match expectations. Sometimes, things do really go wrong (read: tiger shark). But such situations present an opportunity: Learning to cope, making the most of what we've got, is essential to savoring.

"The best savorers can adapt and roll," Bryant said, recalling a time when a massive storm blew in while he was backpacking with a friend. The rain was flooding their campsite, so much so that they became concerned about being able to get out of the woods. Drenched and freezing, they threw everything into the back of their jeep and drove to the nearest motel. When they walked into the lobby, they were sopping and muddy. Guests looked on in silence. And then Bryant's friend broke it:

"We'd like a dry room, please." Everyone erupted in laughter. And that changed everything. "You can still find the joy that is," Bryant said.

On past trips I've been ill and I've lost personal items that were meaningful to me, but none of it was a matter of life or death. Any problems have been of the usual variety: delays, food poisoning, bad weather. When I got lost in Paris on a gray day and ended up at the Musée de Cluny, I decided to make the most of it by exploring the gardens—and along the way discovered the mystery novel, making going astray into a highlight of the trip.

In Üsküdar, I knew I might not be able to see all that I had come for. I was there to visit the Şakirin mosque which, of all the mosques in Istanbul, most captured my imagination with its singular style that brings together the sleek aesthetic of a modern art museum and the spirit and opulence of the Ottoman Empire—an almost futuristic, aluminum dome; arabesque-patterned metal screens; gilded calligraphy—as well as its distinction as being the first mosque interior designed by a woman, Zeynep Fadillioğlu.

"No woman had ever designed a mosque interior, neither in the Ottoman Empire nor in the Turkish Republic, nor to the best of Zeynep's knowledge, anywhere in the world," said the journalist Andrew Finkel in the book I'd read about Fadillioğlu's work. The architect for the project was a man, Hüsrev Tayla, though he collaborated with Fadillioğlu, doing away with side walls and changing the look of the mosque's "welcoming stairs" at her request.

The Şakirin is a neighborhood mosque, not the Blue Mosque, where there's a steady stream of tourists and signs point the way. But after months of anticipating my visit, it was finally time to go, and I accepted the fact that when I arrived, I might not be able to see all that I wanted to see.

From the harbor of Üsküdar, it's about a half-hour walk to the Şakirin, across stone pavers arranged in elaborate patterns—fans, half circles, chevron stripes—under tall trees, past cats sleeping on windowsills. A woman leaned out her apartment window and pulled up a string attached to a bucket with a loaf of bread inside. Damp laundry hung from awning poles, reminiscent of long-ago family afternoons in Brooklyn. I passed a small mosque made of wood, like the delicate pastel *yalis* along the Bosporus. The sloping residential streets were intimate and inviting; tree-lined refuges from the organized chaos at piers and tourist zones.

Outside a marble company, headstones—some with the crescent moon and star of the Turkish flag; others with a Star of David—leaned against a building. Across the street, under soaring cypress trees, Ottoman-style headstones with turban headpieces rose from the edge of a hill on a high wall in the old Karacaahmet Cemetery. I stopped on the sidewalk beside a bed of bright yellow and orange mums, below the cemetery wall, and reached into my bag for a scarf to cover my head. Through the trees I could see a minaret, white, almost chalky blue in the light, with a crescent at its top. On the side of a nearby building, gold letters spelled the name of the mosque that, up until then, I had seen only in the pages of a book: SAKIRIN CAMII. I turned and went up the steps toward the courtyard where in the center was a fountain with a shiny stainless steel sphere symbolizing the universe, reflecting me and everything else around it.

Outside the entrance there were just a few pairs of sandals and sneakers. I stepped out of my shoes and into the dark hall. A couple of women had walked in before me, though by now there was no trace of them. I waited for more to arrive rather than go exploring and inadvertently turn up somewhere I wasn't supposed to be, but no one came. And so I made an educated guess and began slowly walking up the stairs toward the rose-colored dome.

Near the top, whispers trickled down. When I reached them, I found myself in the women's prayer balcony, smaller than the area downstairs where the men were praying, yet open and airy with a prime view of the pink dome above and, below, the turquoise mihrab facing Mecca. The balcony was also closer to the vast three-ring chandelier with its twinkling glass droplets (not unlike those at Ulus 29, the restaurant and club Fadillioğlu helped design) and the sinuous calligraphy of the dome belt, iridescent in the sunlight.

A woman prayed; others watched the men pray beyond the balcony. Children flitted about. A few women spoke softly and laughed without making a sound. One took photos with her smartphone. I stood at the back of the gallery watching, tracing the paths of thin gold lines pinwheeling out from the center of the great pink dome. It looked like an open flower.

After a little while, I went back down the stairs where, at the bottom, a girl with a bob in jeans and a pink T-shirt was barefoot and motionless, peeking around a screen to where men were praying. I was about the same age when I used to eavesdrop on my parents' dinner parties from a balcony in our house. As I reached the last steps, she turned and saw me. I stopped; smiled. I was born in Brooklyn, her sister city.

When preparing for a trip, we can read about architecture and restaurants. But what ultimately breathes life into the daydreams of anticipation are the people we encounter when we're actually there, including those we merely pass on the street or, in this case, the stairwell. I thought, too, of the man on the pier who offered his hand to steady me as I stepped off the ferry, and of the old woman in the public restroom who motioned for me to come and share with her the sole tiny sink. The possibility of these wordless interactions, to which we can be particularly attuned when alone, didn't cross my mind when I was anticipating my days in Istanbul. I had envisioned ships and minarets, the Grand Bazaar and the Hagia Sophia, yet not these faces, not these moments that silently transmit the warmth of a city.

When imagining the mosque, I didn't imagine the things I might pass on my walk there from the harbor: the woman in the window raising a bucket on a string, the men with pushcarts of fruits and vegetables, cats dozing between the flowerpots. These are the street scenes that whisper, the particulars that make a place real, that make a trip our own. The photos of the Şakirin mosque in the coffee table book had appeared more vivid than when I stood before it. And the photographer had zoomed in on design features, creating striking, abstract, images. Yet there was no little girl at the foot of the stairs. There were no women whispering and laughing. What is a place of worship without people? What is Istiklal Avenue, Istanbul's fashionable pedestrian boulevard, without crowds strolling it in the evening, stopping to buy ice cream cones and eat fried fish in the cozy restaurants on its side streets?

To anticipate is to court joy, to fall in love with a place the way it is in a book or a movie or an Eartha Kitt song. But to stay open to the unexpected is to embrace anticipation—to know that it serves its purpose before the journey begins and must then be set aside for reality, for whatever beautiful, strange, unpredictable thing awaits when we step off the ferry.

Outside the mosque, I tied on my sneakers and made my way through the courtyard where patterned screens threw arabesque shadows on the ground, past the mums, the cemetery, and the cypress trees, back to the harbor, to a ferry full of people, on our way to yet another shore.

# The Hamam

*The Importance of Trying New Things*

*In order to allow for creative self-renewal and growth, it's
really advisable to go outside the boundaries of what you do
and expose yourself to alien worlds as much as possible.*

—Hussein Chalayan, fashion designer

So there was the matter of the hamam.

"Oh, you must go," said my friend John, a seasoned traveler, back in New York. "You *must*."

Must I? I was longing to see the architecture, but I wasn't longing to have a treatment. I'm not a big bath- or spa-goer, be it a hot spring or a hamam. Besides, I'd read Mark Twain, who'd long fantasized about the romance of the Turkish bath: its tranquility, its fragrant spices, its "music of fountains that counterfeited the pattering of summer rain," as he wrote in his nineteenth-century satirical travelogue *The Innocents Abroad*. When at last he was able to experience it firsthand, he found himself naked with soap in his eyes, being scrubbed head to heels by an unforgiving man with a coarse mitten.

"He bore hard on his mitten, and from under it rolled little cylinders, like maccaroni," Twain wrote. "It could not be dirt, for it was too white. He pared me down in this way for a long time. Finally I said: 'It is a tedious process. It will take hours to trim me to the size you want me; I will wait; go and borrow a jack-plane.'"

Thus was realized Twain's dream of Eastern bliss. As was that of the Italian novelist Edmondo De Amicis, who about a decade later warned that prior to entering a hamam one ought to ask oneself, *Quid valeant humeri*—in short, "how much my shoulders can bear"—because not everyone is capable of enduring the experience. During his own scrub, De Amicis found himself wondering "whether I shouldn't start to lash out with a punch or a slap and defend myself as best I can."

Twain and De Amicis were obviously writing to entertain their respective audiences. Yet their accounts, as over-the-top as they were, triggered practical questions for a reluctant spagoer: *How vigorous is the modern scrub? How cold is the water? How many people would see me—and in what state of undress?*

Days before my flight to Istanbul, however, these and other trivialities were overshadowed by the State Department emails landing in my in-box. "Be alert to the possibility of increased terror activity in urban and tourist areas," read one email. It was just after members of the Revolutionary People's Liberation Party/Front, or D.H.K.P./C., a Marxist-Leninist group, had opened fire at the consulate building in Istanbul. "Terrorists can conduct complex attacks," the email said, "with secondary follow-on attacks."

A year earlier, Istanbul had been ranked the most popular

travel destination in the world by the industry behemoth TripAdvisor. A few years before that, the *Guardian* called it "the new party capital of Europe." Its nightclubs are storied. John F. Kennedy, Jr., and Carolyn Bessette Kennedy honeymooned there. It's where Hemingway cut his teeth writing dispatches during the Greco-Turkish war, and where James Baldwin finished writing *Another Country*. It's been the backdrop to novels and travelogues by Agatha Christie and Ian Fleming, and a vacation destination for Greta Garbo, Josephine Baker, Bono, and Oprah. Istanbul was the capital of the Byzantine and Ottoman Empires. It's the land of the Bosporus, the Blue Mosque, and the Grand Bazaar—and after years of my longing to go, it was finally happening.

Then came the State Department emails. I took them seriously. At the same time, anyone who lives in a major city—be it New York, Paris, or Istanbul—knows that while attacks can and have happened, for the most part daily life is peaceful. When I was readying for Istanbul, the string of bombings and shootings that would send the city reeling later that year and throughout 2016 had yet to really begin. Thousands of citizens had not yet been purged in the wake of an attempted coup. In the summer of 2015, Istanbul beckoned. My husband, whom I was dating at the time, had plans to meet colleagues there, and I had spent months contemplating my solitary itineraries. And so when the State Department emails arrived, I read them carefully (they weren't specific; they simply advised Americans to be vigilant) and then boarded a plane to Turkey, where the summer days and nights were lazy and picturesque. I sampled flavorful spreads and meats, and sipped cold beer while gazing at bridges lit up across the Bosporus. I walked Istiklal Avenue behind a slow red trolley with a young man in Nike sneakers hanging off the back. I stopped into shops and upscale malls like Akmerkez, where a rooftop terrace offered swings, deck chairs, table tennis, and little booths shaped like houses for quiet conversation. I climbed Ulus park for a gull's-eye view of the Bosporus, and strolled along seaside *yalis* with fast-melting ice cream. And one morning, after Turkish coffee and a croque madame, I took a tram to the old city and approached the steps of the Cemberlitas hamam. Above the entrance were the words "Built by Mimar Sinan in 1584."

I stood apart from the stream of customers. Must we do things that make us uncertain or uncomfortable? Science suggests that activities that lead us to feel uncertainty and discomfort "are associated with some of the most memorable and enjoyable experiences of people's lives," as the psychologists Robert Biswas-Diener and Todd B. Kashdan wrote in *Psychology Today*. Memorable, certainly, but are they genuinely enjoyable? The researchers found that joyful and fulfilled people seem to intuitively know "that sustained happiness is not just about doing things that you like. It also requires growth and adventuring beyond the boundaries of your comfort zone." Happy people, they said, are curious people. Without curiosity, Kashdan explains in the *Oxford Handbook of Positive Psychology*, we would not explore both ourselves and the world, would not engage in a search for any meaning in life, and would have no foundation for aesthetic appreciation, scientific pursuits, or innovation.

Even when the outcome isn't what we hoped it would be,

making the effort to experience something new can still be good for us. It can help us think of ourselves as the kind of people who are capable of taking action, as Lyubomirsky has written. Plus, she said, it can whet our appetite for future risks. These risks need not be major. Simply getting out of our comfort zones—trying a different route to work, introducing ourselves to a new neighbor, speaking up for something we believe in—is important, she found, because it can help us spot opportunities, discover a strength, and shape the trajectory of our life rather than regretting our inaction.

I stepped up to a sign that described the hamam's three twenty-first-century offerings:

> TRADITIONAL STYLE. Includes 15 minutes body scrub & bubble wash by your attendant and afterwards you may bathe yourself again and rest on the marble platform as long as you like.
> LUXURY STYLE. Includes 15 minutes body scrub & bubble wash + 30 minutes oil massage on the table and afterwards you may bathe yourself again and rest on the marble platform as long as you like.
> SELF SERVICE. You may bathe yourself and rest on the marble platform as long as you like.

A booklet prepared by the hamam explained that a good scrub reduces stress, keeps skin young and smooth, alleviates muscle aches, and increases circulation as well as "the happiness hormone." I was willing to forgo the happiness hormone in favor of an option that didn't include the words "body scrub."

There was only one: Self Service, a choice that travel guides caution tourists against because no instruction is offered about what to do on your own. That lack of direction might seem perilous when, say, bungee jumping, but how complicated could a bath be?

Besides, while Cemberlitas is a classical hamam, it's exceedingly tourist-friendly. A copy of *Time Out Istanbul* in my hotel room called it and its ilk a "decaf version" of a Turkish bath. The list of services was written in English and Spanish. And there was a F.A.Q. sign with essential questions such as "Are there any hairdryers?" (Yes.)

I paid 60 Turkish lira (about $17 U.S. dollars at the time) and almost instantly regretted it, because in return I was handed a large red card that said SELF SERVICE. I was also given a key; a small, thin, striped towel known as a *pestemal*; and a sparkly drawstring bag with a pair of black underwear inside. A woman pointed upstairs. I followed her finger with relief and a dash of hubris at being offered directions despite my big red SELF SERVICE sign.

Within seconds I blew by my dressing room, mistakenly walking up too many steps. Another woman directed me back down where, on the way, I passed a visitor in a *pestemal*—a fortunate encounter, because I now knew what to do with mine. (The F.A.Q. sign actually tells visitors exactly what to do, but I was so distracted that while I looked at the sign, I didn't read it).

There was a natural beauty and simplicity to the pale wood stairs and changing rooms. Inside one, I wrapped as much of myself as would fit under the *pestemal* (not much), then emerged to put my clothes in a locker and follow more pointed fingers past women in towels sipping tea, waiting for manicures and pedicures, until I reached a small room.

Where was the big heated platform? Where was the dome? I turned around to ask, but no one was there. Perhaps those who selected Self Service were sent to a no-frills area of the hamam. There was a shower and a little room with a massage table. What was I supposed to be doing? WHY did I choose Self Service?

I noticed a large wooden door and considered the possibility that on the other side of it might be a woman in the midst of a private massage. Or even a man. I stood looking at the door, trying to will someone to come out. But there's only so much time you can spend standing around in a towel. Finally, I went through.

———

Steam.

Echoes of falling water.

I'd found the hot room. Soaring columns held up a vast dome. In the center was the large marble platform, the *gobek tasi*, on which a handful of women were lying. But it was not this platform, or even the tall white columns, like old, petrified trees, that gave the space its magic. It was the scattered glass "elephant eyes," as the openings in the dome are called. They allowed long, hazy shafts of daylight to pour in, down to the marble pedestal, over bare arms and legs, like sunlight falling through the canopy of a dense forest.

A few of the women were being scrubbed. It didn't look particularly vigorous. One woman near the door was on her back, feet dangling off the platform, a loofah in one hand, resting on her chest.

It was unclear to me whether the protocol was to wash in one of the bathing cubicles before or after lying on the slab. Maybe it was both. In my zeal to research the bath's history, I'd neglected to read up on the present. (I decided to do both, though I later learned that guests are encouraged to sweat and then wash.) After a quick rinse, I laid my *pestemal* between two women and stretched out.

Heat radiated from under the marble, seeped through the towel, into my back and arms. I pressed my shoulders, which in New York are generally perched up around my ears, into the stone and looked up, as if under a hazy night sky. The dome was ringed by six-pointed stars. Steam and dust floated in the slender rays of light falling toward us.

I closed my eyes and listened to nearby whispers and watery echoes, feeling a kind of silent kinship with the other women on the marble. My mind drifted back to a summer afternoon near the Delaware River where in my twenties I came across a copy of Gloria Steinem's *Outrageous Acts and Everyday Rebellions* in a used-book shop. A chapter called "In Praise of Women's Bodies" begins with a question: "How long has it been since you spent a few days in the intimate company of women: dressing and undressing, talking, showering, resting—the kind of casual togetherness that seems more common to locker rooms of men?"

In my case it had, in fact, been years. Steinem was advocating for diverse, unselfconscious togetherness, for women to find time to be with their own bodies and those of other women when they aren't on display for men.

I opened my eyes and looked around. Women were lying on their stomachs being scrubbed by attendants with buckets of soapy water. Some were off on their own, washing under the arcade. Others lounged on the warm marble. No one seemed to pay any mind to what anyone else was doing, let alone to what they looked like.

I sat up, swung my legs over the edge of the platform, and wandered back to a washing station. I turned a handle on the faucet, released a little hot water, then a little cool, swirled them together in a pretty copper bowl, and tipped it over my shoulder. The sound of water filling the metal bowl, the weight of the bowl in my hands, the act of raising it above my head and pouring water over my shoulder instead of standing under the steady flow of a showerhead—it was a ritual at once ancient and new. I filled the bowl again.

Social scientists have found that new experiences tend to make us more intensely happy than new things. One reason why is that unlike material objects, experiences help prevent a psychological phenomenon known as hedonic adaptation— our ability to swiftly adapt to whatever happens to us and return to our own typical level of happiness. While that ability is a powerful survival tool, in daily life, adaptation can lead to boredom. The pleasure of owning a new bracelet may fade with familiarity, but a performance by whirling dervishes, for example, is not likely something we'd adapt to, even if we saw it every day, because the dance is never quite the same.

We're also less likely to compare our experiences (as opposed to our material possessions) with those of other people, which in turn staves off a keeping-up-with-the-Joneses mentality. If you and a friend went on separate Caribbean vacations, and if your friend's account of his trip sounded better than yours, it still wouldn't bother you nearly as much as if you went to his house and saw that he had a bigger, sleeker television than the one you just bought, "because you have your memories," Thomas Gilovich of Cornell University told the *Cornell Chronicle*. "It's your idiosyncratic connection to the Caribbean that makes it your vacation. That makes it less comparable to mine, hence your enjoyment isn't undermined as much."

Of course, having new experiences and trying novel things doesn't magically endow us with confidence. But it can begin the process by demonstrating to ourselves that we're capable. It allows us to look back and say, *I did that*. We don't need proverbs, because we have proof.

Outward Bound, the organization founded in 1941 that offers wilderness and other educational programs, is known for giving participants the opportunity to "solo"—to go off alone and reflect on the journey they've just completed. For many students, the solo is the highlight of their experience, the organization has said, and that after the course, students report higher levels of confidence and self-esteem.

Walking back to the locker after the hot room, I had a tingling, bodily calm, and an unexpected feeling of gentleness toward the women I encountered along the way. I retrieved my clothes and slipped into a changing stall. I wasn't necessarily leaving with a dewy glow, but with renewed appreciation for the skins we inhabit. When I came out, a woman pointed at a bin.

I dropped the towel in, and returned to the city.

# Call to Prayer

## Learning to Listen

*The sounds bore an invitation.*

—Ahmet Hamdi Tanpinar, *A Mind at Peace*

The voice of the muezzin echoed across Ortaköy pier and out to sea. It crackled through loudspeakers on the minarets, over the women in black abayas with pink iPhones on selfie sticks, the men in polo shirts on white yachts bobbing in the water, like the ghostly jellyfish between them.

A small, cheerful crowd was taking photographs at the lip of the Bosporus on the sliver of land between the suspension bridge built in 1973 and the Baroque-style Ortaköy mosque, designed by Nigoğos Balyan (who worked on the sprawling Dolmabahçe Palace, one of the city's top tourist destinations, as well).

People strolled along brick paths under banners of Turkish flags strung from one lamppost to the next, past umbrellas and tents with tables where merchants were selling blue evil eyes (*nazar*) and hand of Fatima charms the size of door knockers.

Children climbed plastic slides in a play area with public telephones shaped like dolphins, while their grandparents licked ice cream cones on benches in the shade of trees. No one stopped for the muezzin. His cry was but one more sound among many on the pier on a summer afternoon.

It came like an ache, like a song, like a yearning before sunrise, at bedtime, and three times in between. It was the *adhan*, the call to prayer by a man in a tower (or, as it can be these days, a recording).

All cities have their soundscapes, their particular symphony. In New York, subways scream as they pull into stations and jackhammers ring in the morning. And still, we manage to read our books and finish complex projects with the necessary concentration. Yet the *adhan* and its haunting melisma went over and in me, stopping my thoughts until the voice was gone and the air shivered in silence. Over the course of several days it became for me, Western and secular, a kind of call to solitude—"a bell of mindfulness," to borrow a phrase from the Buddhist monk Thich Nhat Hanh. Several times a day it snapped me back into the moment when I was distracted by heat or a tough walk up one of the city's hills, which in August was nearly every walk.

"Every time we hear the bell," Nhat Hanh wrote in *Peace Is Every Step*, "we stop talking, stop our thinking, and return to ourselves." The monks pause, he said. They breathe. When they inhale they sometimes say, *Listen, listen*.

In the old city, calls to prayer wash over the teeming Eminönü pier. People pour off boats, everyone with somewhere to be or someone to meet.

Women rolling luggage stopped to buy the *Hurriyet* and *Daily Sabah* newspapers under a red umbrella advertising Coca-Cola. Tourists in shorts ate fish sandwiches on low stools in boat restaurants with little golden domes. Men sold corn cobs for 2 lira; children bought *simit* from pushcarts with red-and-white-striped awnings; fishermen dangled rods over the Bosporus; couples on benches looked out at the sea; a man in an orange vest swept the plaza. Gulls circled them all.

Eminönü is among the city's busiest ferry stops, though each stop features its colorful port scenes: men selling flowers from pushcarts and tents; white-haired shoe shiners sitting behind their brass boxes under trees and umbrellas; yellow taxis idling at the curb. Nearby, the clock towers of the Sirkeci Terminal, once the final stop on the Orient Express, rose beside an empty train car. The domes of vast mosques shined in the sunlight.

"I liked to be alone in Constantinople," Greta Garbo told *Photoplay* magazine in 1928. "I was not lonely." She walked around the old city mostly by herself, explaining, "It is not necessary to have company when you travel."

In the old city, there is plenty of company. I melted into the crowd descending into a tunnel under a busy road and was carried along past stalls selling headphones, sandals, and plastic toys. At the far end I climbed more stairs back out into the heat, heading south to the ancient arcades of the Grand Bazaar.

I'd pictured finding there labyrinthine corridors piled with spices and handmade textiles you couldn't buy anywhere else. And so I felt naive when at last I reached a vast stone gate to one of the world's oldest markets and saw that it was flanked by displays of plastic sunglasses, like the entrance to a Times

Square gift shop. A door fit for a giant was partly covered with Istanbul magnets, some shaped like whirling dervishes, others doing double duty as golden beer bottle openers. But of course the bazaar had such trifles; it wasn't the fifteenth century.

Inside, under the vaulted ceilings, things got more interesting. Everything mingled: the old, new, cheap, extravagant. There were hills of spices and dried fruit—apricots, mulberries, mangos, grapefruits, pineapples, strawberries, ginger, cranberries—and bins of colorful tea in flavors like kiwi, lemon, apple, and orange. There were boxes of *lokum* (Turkish delight) flavored with fig-walnut and apricot, almond and honey. There were baskets filled with pastries the color of pale roses, and glass display cases with even more *lokum,* this time formed into logs, and in more variations of pistachio flavors than I knew possible: grape pistachio, milk pistachio, honey pistachio.

In the maze of covered streets, merchants called out as I passed, pools of light illuminating gold bangles, scarves, ceramics, and hookahs for sale. Many of the shops were not unlike mall boutiques, with electric signs, glass storefronts, and shelves of accessories and housewares.

Outdoors, under tarps and awnings, were entire streets lined with stalls selling cookware and household sundries (brooms, feather dusters, honey wands). Some of the items, whether an economy-size pack of sponges or a wood chair, dangled like piñatas from ropes above shoppers' heads.

I'd expected the bazaar to feel different from other places I'd gone browsing, yet having come from a mall and Walmart culture, saturated with name brands and knockoffs alike, I was on familiar ground among the clothes and sneakers displayed beside signs that advertised Tommy Hilfiger and Ralph Lauren.

Next to a crumbling wall, up a short flight of steps adjacent to the Grand Bazaar, the Sahaflar Carsisi (or Old Book Bazaar) is comparatively tiny, a quiet square ringed by low-slung bookshops. Turkish flags were tacked to tree trunks and hung here and there from stalls and tables chock-a-block with novels, dictionaries, textbooks, and pens.

Seeing the textbooks deepened my desire to visit Istanbul University, a five-minute walk away, but there was only so much time, and it was in the opposite direction of a place I simply had to see: the Basilica Cistern.

A vast underground lake built in the sixth century to store water that flowed from woods north of Istanbul, the Cistern, I had envisioned, was the city's romantic haunted house. The nineteenth-century French poet and journalist Théophile Gautier described it as grim and lugubrious. He imagined that the boats that used to glide on its black waters never returned, as if led to Hades by the boatman of the Styx, and he said the Turks believed the Cistern was populated with djinns and ghouls. I couldn't wait.

Steps lead down from the sunbaked streets, plunging visitors into exquisite darkness beneath vaulted stone arcades on the banks of a subterranean sea. Hundreds of ancient marble columns extend on into the abyss, illuminated only by small lamps at the base that gave the effect of candlelight. It was as eerie as I'd hoped.

Bridges carried visitors over mysterious fish circling in the water. I followed the columns deeper into the dark, along ramps to where the crowd had come to a stop in a dead end in the northwest corner of the Cistern. There, like a treasure in an Indiana Jones film, sat two large stone Medusa heads. No one knows how they got there. "It is said that in the old times the statues and pictures of Medusa were placed in very important buildings and private places to keep them away from bad omens," suggests a sign. Travel guides and articles talk about the frightfulness of these heads, which every few minutes were illuminated by someone's camera flash. One of the stone faces, upside down in shallow water, has full, soft-looking cheeks and a pudgy chin. Frightful? She looks like someone's grandmother about to nod off for a nap. The other head is on its side and has a wavy lock of hair that seems to be a snake, but even so, it appears to be the suburban garden variety rather than the sort likely to inflict a mortal wound.

Why Medusa had snakes for hair and could turn men to stone, whether she was a woman or a monster, both or neither, depends on whatever tale you happen to read. In Edith Hamilton's classic telling, Medusa was one of three winged monsters, the "Terrible Sisters" known as Gorgons, who lived on an island. Covered in gold scales, with twisting snakes for hair, Medusa was the only mortal member of the trio. Yet she was able to instantly turn anyone to stone with her gaze. A billboard at the Cistern offered another theory: Medusa was born beautiful, proud of her long hair and lovely body. She was in love with the son of Zeus, Perseus. Unfortunately for her, so was Athena, goddess of wisdom, who in an ungenerous moment turned Medusa's prized hair into snakes. (In Hamilton's version, the first time Perseus encounters Medusa she's already a monster and he has come to behead her.) The heads in the Cistern were gentle-looking, hardly forbidding, and not as large as I had imagined.

When we initially encounter a place or object, in a book or on a computer screen, it's necessary to guard against allowing the image to become the real thing. "The copy," as the scholar and novelist Umberto Eco put it, "seems more convincing than the model." Of course, I was doing precisely what research tells us not to do: I had set my expectations for the Medusa heads in stone. And so there in the dark, away from the heads, I stopped to consider how remarkable it was to be thousands of miles from home in a subterranean vault with enigmatic statues— possibly guarding against ancient omens—beneath the bustling streets of a majestic city.

From the depths of the Cistern I climbed back to the bright street and wandered over to nearby Sultanahmet Arkeolojik Park, between the Hagia Sophia and the Blue Mosque, an area of the old city that can feel like strolling through Eco's ultimate hyperreality. There were long lines of tourists, the murmur of shooting fountains, manicured lawns with decorative gold edging, chattering children dressed as sultans, young men stopping passersby to sell carpets, women scrolling through photos on their cameras, and booths loaning free head scarves and clothes to cover up bare shoulders and legs before entering the Blue Mosque. Add to all this the sudden wail of a muezzin, invisible, like the shimmering heat.

The muezzin called the faithful to prayer on a summer afternoon, just as another muezzin before him had done, and one before him, stretching back in time. On that summer afternoon, though, there wasn't only a single voice—but one from the north, and one from the south. *Listen, listen.*

Outside the Hagia Sophia, children whipped their heads this way and that, toward whichever direction they heard the adhan. When one muezzin would pause, the other would take up his call. Their staggered voices echoed back and forth between the Hagia Sophia and the Blue Mosque, through the palm and Erguvan trees, through me.

Alone, we can listen, not to those who tell us we must see the famous this or that, or to the voice in our head that says a place must be as it seems in a film or on a website—but to what's really there. We can hear the muezzin, the bookseller, the rug hawker, the echoes of an ancient cistern and the mysteries buried within. Alone, we don't have to speak. We can feel the vibration of a city as it is in that moment in time and will never be again: the sound of the crowd, the waves crashing into the harbor, the cries of seagulls swooping over the Bosporus.

Here, and then gone.

# LOSS

# The Rainbow Stairs of Beyoğlu

*Appreciation*

> *Some day in the future we will remember the here and now.*
> —Orhan Pamuk, *The Innocence of Objects*

On the tumbledown stairs between the Bosporus and Cihangir were two black crows and a pack of skeletal cats. The cats looked pitifully hungry. The crows, on the contrary, were plump, their feathers as shiny and black as an oil slick. Their sharp beaks held berries plucked from the plastic tub they had gathered around like a bar cart, making them seem partly human, like the Surrealist painter Leonora Carrington's *Crow Catcher*.

The stairs, or what was left of them, had their own strangeness. They were painted rainbow colors that had long since faded. Weeds poked through the cracks. In some places, entire chunks of the steps had disintegrated, so that all that remained was a patch of the hill on which they were built. Later, I would learn that these faded rainbow steps are known as the Findikli stairs. In 2013, a retired forestry engineer named Huseyin Cetinel spent four days painting them in what the *New York Times* described as "an act of guerrilla beautification." The project cost him about $800 in paint. Asked why he did it, he said, "To make people smile."

It worked. Istanbullis from other neighborhoods flocked to the steps. They sat on them. They climbed them. They took pictures in front of them as if posing in front of the Taj Mahal. But before long, government workers came and painted the stairs back to battleship gray, sparking protests across Turkey, and on Twitter. A hashtag was born: #DirenMerdiven, or #Resist-Stairs. Other neighborhoods painted their own staircases rainbow colors in solidarity. There was such a ruckus that the government eventually relented, and the Findikli stairs were returned to their rainbow state.

Faded now, they had all the frightful beauty of a fairy tale as I began to climb them, eyes averted, hoping not to draw the attention of the crows. I slipped by, past a wall topped with barbed wire, toward the muffled sounds of domestic life, un-seen, from open windows.

"Who knows what web of gossip and intrigue you have momentarily disturbed?" De Amicis wrote in the nineteenth century about walking streets like this. "You see no one, but a thousand eyes see you."

Halfway up the steep hill, I stopped to slow my heart, thumping from the climb in the heat. Young men were perched on the next flight of stairs as if they were spectators in an amphitheater, looking down upon the city. Beyond them were even more stairs, leading where I couldn't see. But somewhere at the top, wherever that might be, was my destination: Cihangir, a neighborhood that's home to writers and artists.

I rounded a bend, past a playground with a young man asleep on a slide in the sun, and entered a maze of gray staircases and empty passageways, everything cracked and blooming. Now and then I'd be hemmed in between apartment buildings with the inevitable satellite dishes beside their windows, wires dangling like Rapunzel's hair. Some buildings looked as if a creature had come in the night and nibbled their corners.

From a distance, these backstreets and alleys in the valleys between towers and minarets are invisible. But up close and inside, they have a certain poetry that seems to exemplify the Japanese notion of *wabi-sabi,* of seeing beauty in simple, earthy things that are imperfect and fleeting: the remains of a graffitied wall revealing large old stones beneath it; green tendrils peeking over walls. "*Wabi-sabi* is a beauty of things imperfect, impermanent and incomplete," writes the designer and writer Leonard Koren in his meditation on the subject. *Wabi-sabi,* he says, can spring from "a sad-beautiful feeling," a kind of melancholy: "The mournful quarks and caws of seagulls and crows. The forlorn bellowing of foghorns." Orhan Pamuk used the Turkish word *huzun* to describe his city's communal melancholy in his novel *Istanbul,* just as his fellow countryman Ahmet Hamdi Tanpinar did more than half a century earlier in *A Mind at Peace. Huzun* is a feeling, a heartache, as Pamuk puts it; something he said could be seen in Istanbul in an ancient clock tower, an old postcard seller, a fisherman heading out to sea, neglected mosques, "everything being broken, worn out, past its prime."

I made my way up ever more stairs, with ever more walls

rising on either side of me. At the top of yet another hill—or was it the same one?—I stepped out expecting another alleyway but instead found myself next to a large potted oleander on a wide, tree-lined boulevard. There were restaurants and sidewalk tables with checkered cloths and café chairs. Coffee shops had clapboard menus on the curb. It was as if I had emerged from another dimension, another time, like a character in a Haruki Murakami novel.

It was afternoon in Cihangir. Stores were selling takeaway *affogato* and smoothies, antiques, used books, and home accessories. Workers and owners sat outside their shops on chairs and benches. The doors and windows to the cafés were open wide, inviting in the last weeks of summer. Inside, young people typed on laptops while listening to music. Michael Jackson's "Thriller" trailed me up the street. Near a mosque with a slim white minaret was a sign with an arrow pointing toward the "Museum of Innocence." I followed it.

The sloping brick streets meandered through the neighborhood, past storefronts, some covered with ivy, others that seemed to have displayed more of their wares on the sidewalk— postcards, books, hats—than on their shelves. On one brick street a jumble of antique furniture was lined up along the curb. Painted canvasses, presumably for sale, leaned and hung on the wall of a building and then, just past an alley sprouting weeds, rose a slim, burnt-red townhouse with a red banner—I'd arrived at the museum.

Despite the sign, the place looked as if it would have preferred not to have been found, for it was clapped down like a ship in a storm. The windows were shuttered, and there wasn't so much as a sign on the door on Çukurcuma Caddesi. It took a moment for me to realize the ticket window was around the corner. I stepped up to the counter, paid the 25 lira (about $7 dollars) entry fee, and opened a door into the dark.

The Museum of Innocence is a place, but it's also the title of a novel by the Nobel laureate Orhan Pamuk. In it, the protagonist, Kemal, creates a museum to house the artifacts he has spent years collecting from and about his beloved, Fusun, who, as these things sometimes go in epic love stories, ended up marrying another man. Pamuk conceived of both the museum and the novel at the same time, though the book appeared first, in 2008. The museum opened four years later.

It was a dormitory for local workers when Pamuk bought the building, with garbage in its doorway and even along the edge of the house, under a sign that warned "No trashing." When I showed up that summer afternoon more than fifteen years later, it was immaculate.

Visitors are told that the townhouse is Fusun's former home. In eighty-three vitrines on the walls are everyday sundries from Istanbul life in the latter half of the twentieth century (a dress, a watch) grouped in accordance with the chapters in Pamuk's book. These objects, a museum booklet tells visitors, were "used, worn, heard, seen, collected and dreamt of by the characters in the novel."

The centerpiece of the entrance hall is a black-and-white spiral on the floor, meant to signify Time. It can be seen from each floor of the townhouse if you lean ever so slightly over the central stairwell. Yet even if the spiral weren't there, it would be hard to forget time in this place. The museum has many beautiful timepieces: a grandfather clock, an alarm clock, a pocket watch; clocks with pendulums, clocks with chimes. In certain corners you could hear a soft ticking, each second, each breath, noted, and gone. Between transparent panes were all kinds of old keys, as if they had rained from the sky and froze when time suddenly stopped.

In the novel, Kemal suggests that remembering Time is often painful, because it's linear and eventually comes to an end. And so he proposes that we try to stop thinking of that Aristotelian notion of Time and instead cherish it for each of its deepest moments. Every object in the museum, for instance, is meant to preserve and celebrate a happy moment with Fusun. No item is too insignificant. Consider box 68: an almost entomological display of 4,213 cigarette butts, each inhaled and snuffed out by Fusun, pinned to a wall like butterflies in a natural history museum.

A faint glow from the vitrines offers little light on each floor so that visitors are aware that it's daytime only from the sunlight seeping in through gaps around the shuttered windows. The top floor is an exception. Hanging on the walls are pages from Pamuk's original manuscript, handwritten in Turkish with strikethroughs, stains, drawings, and doodles. On one of these pages is the first line of the novel: "It was the happiest moment of my life, though I didn't know it" was written in 2002 while Pamuk was visiting the New York Public Library on Fifth Avenue.

Wandering the dark floors of Pamuk's imagination, you

can't help but feel nostalgic. And perhaps a little sorrowful. Every relic, every object, got me thinking about what the theorist Roland Barthes said about photographs in "Camera Lucida": You can look at them and say, *"That* is dead and *that* is going to die." Like the plaster cast of Chopin's hand in the Musée de la Vie Romantique, what good is it without the man?

Even though the objects in the Museum of Innocence were meant to commemorate happy moments, I felt blue behind the shuttered windows with the remnants of a life. It didn't matter that Fusun and Kemal weren't real. Kemal feels like a proxy for all of us, for what we try to keep; for what we eventually lose. It's not hard, standing in the townhouse, to picture yourself growing older, losing people you love, feeling betrayed by solitude.

By the time I had finished looking at the marked-up manuscript, I was itching to rejoin the world. I followed the stairs back down to the Time spiral in the entryway and out into the late afternoon sun, grateful to feel it on my face, to leave the shadow boxes, to be walking (downhill!) to the glittering Bosporus, to the streets alive with people, to everything I hadn't lost.

# Before It's Gone

## *Ephemeralities*

> *The morning*
> *wind spreads its*
> *fresh smell.*
> *We must get up*
> *and take that in,*
> *that wind that*
> *lets us live.*
> *Breathe before*
> *it's gone.*
>
> —Rumi

The week before I arrived in Istanbul, I was commuting to Times Square with its jackhammers, sirens, and Citi Bikes, the man in a Mickey Mouse costume carrying his furry head across 42nd Street like a bowling ball, flocks of pigeons missing toes, giant flashing screens, droplets that splashed onto your head from what you prayed were air conditioners.

I had just finished reading Pico Iyer's *The Art of Stillness*, in which he writes about Leonard Cohen, the singer and song-writer who spent more than five years in a monastery in California. The book put me in the mood for Cohen's deep, gravelly voice, which is how I ended up spending several morning commutes listening to "Hallelujah" on repeat, keeping pace with horses pulling empty carriages, all of us clomping east.

It was only days later that I was ascending the steps of the Istanbul Modern museum, more than five thousand miles away. On one side was the beautiful, broken-down Tophane clock tower—the oldest of its kind in Istanbul, according to the *Daily Sabah*—beside leafy trees that looked as if one day they might try and swallow the clock whole. A few feet away, a tall red pillar announced ISTANBUL MODERN, previewing the museum's industrial aesthetic, with the exposed ductwork and big windows of the old warehouse that's now home to works by leading contemporary artists.

Among the first things I saw when I entered was a video installation called *Undressing*. In it, the Istanbul-born artist Nilbar Gures was hidden under layers of head scarves. She removed them one by one, reciting the names of women she knew in an effort to show, as she put it, that they are individuals, not representations of particular countries, or Islam, or "religious or nationalist ideas."

As she peeled away the scarves, I heard in the distance a faint *hallelujah*. It was soft—so soft that it was nearly inaudible; the echo of a summer morning heard halfway around the world.

*Hallelujah* . . .

I walked toward it, deeper into the museum.

*Hallelujah* . . .

It wasn't Leonard Cohen's voice, though it was his song.

I followed the voice, past a series of black-and-white photographs by Yildiz Moran, the first female photographer in Turkey to receive academic training, as a sign explained. Toward the back of the museum, I found the source of the music: a speaker in a plastic dome hanging from the ceiling. It looked like something George Jetson might use to beam from his garage to his living room. I stood beneath it.

*Hallelujah* . . .

The song was part of a video installation called *I Can Sing* (2008) by the Turkish artist Ferhat Özgür. It had been included in his solo exhibition in New York at MoMA in 2013, but this was my first time seeing it. The video shows an Anatolian woman in a head scarf lip-synching to Jeff Buckley's cover of "Hallelujah" amid a rising housing development on a road to an airport. Something about the song, the place, the woman facing the camera and lip-synching, made me tear up. The video, the wall text said, with its female figure and male voice, its traditional attire and Western music, is meant to show "conflicting feelings of grief and joy and of approval and resistance in the face of change."

> *I heard there was a secret chord*
> *That David played and it pleased the lord*

I wandered away from *I Can Sing,* looking at other works, like one by the fashion designer Hussein Chalayan, which used recordings of cries from seagulls—the city's eternal residents,

145

as he once put it. Still, I could hear "Hallelujah." I went over to the chic Istanbul Modern café and restaurant at the far side of the floor and asked for a table on the deck along the water.

From a rattan chair beside the Bosporus, across from the domes that bloom on the Golden Horn, I ordered a plate of homemade spinach and cheese ravioli. The waiter brought over a wire basket filled with toasted flatbreads and rolls, and a small bowl of spiced oil with black olives and fennel seeds. To my right, through the restaurant window, was a man eating by himself and writing in a notebook. To my left was the steel-blue Bosporus. The ships came and went, but the refrain remained.

*Hallelujah.*

---

My last day in Istanbul there was an attack west of my hotel, at the Dolmabahçe Palace, part of the unrest between leftist militants and Turkish forces, news reports said. A grenade had been thrown; shots had been fired at the guards. The assailants, two men with an automatic weapon, ammunition, and hand grenades, had been arrested. No one had been killed.

Five months later, a young Islamic State operative from Syria walked into the central historic district that's home to the Blue Mosque and Cemberlitas hamam, and detonated a vest of explosives. Ten tourists were killed, and more than a dozen were wounded. It was the beginning of a wave of violence.

Hours before the Dolmabahçe Palace attack, I was leaving my hotel. It was another warm, sunny morning. My taxi pulled out of the gates and within moments it was passing the Dolmabahçe Palace, the ferry terminal to Üsküdar, the Istanbul Modern.

In the museum, next to the video where "Hallelujah" played, there was an installation titled *Bring Yourself to Me* (2009) by the artist Handan Borutecene. It was a jumble of brown chairs with African masks on them, suitcases once carried by migrants to France from Turkey, and magnifying glasses dating from 1890 through 1960. The chairs were from the Palais de la Porte Dorée in Paris, which has been home to various ethnological museums. Visitors were encouraged to use the magnifiers to examine the markings on the suitcases, and wall text explained that the piece was part of a meditation on how immigration can enrich a nation. Also on the wall was a reference to a poem by Rumi. "How good to migrate anew everyday," the English translation said. "And how beautiful to settle anew everyday."

The taxi sped toward the airport, where I had arrived only a few days earlier. It was from a taxi that I would first and last see the Bosporus. It was glittering in the late afternoon sun on the day I landed. Shirtless sunbathers were stretched out on the seawalls. Every so often traffic came to a standstill, and wiry men descended onto the highway, weaving among the cars, selling water, roses, wooden bows and arrows, wheat stalks, car chargers, toy motorcycles, *simit* on platters miraculously balanced on their heads. When traffic began to move again, they receded like the tide.

Now the road was leading away from the Istanbul Modern, away from the broken clock tower, the rainbow stairs, and the girl with the pink shirt in the quiet mosque on the Asia side of the Bosporus. "So many words that belong to yesterday," said the Rumi poem. "Now we need to say new things."

In the coming months there would be terrorist attacks

throughout Turkey: in tourist areas, at private celebrations, during sporting events. Yet they would be outnumbered by the days that were quiet and still. The bazaar opens its gates. The ferries zip back and forth.

I thought about the people and places I had seen, and the many more I hadn't, and hoped to one day see. And I thought about how we are lucky to catch whatever we can, for however long we have, in peace, under a blue sky, in late summer.

## PART III

Fall

# Florence

# SILENCE

# Arrows and Angels

*Games for One*

*Thou must be like a promontory of the sea, against which though the waves beat continually, yet it both itself stands, and about it are those swelling waves stilled and quieted.*
—Marcus Aurelius, *Meditations*

The path was edged with leaves, tawny, crisp, curled at the edges. The trees glowed yellow in the sunlight, like the farmhouses on the hillside. Were it not for the color of the foliage you could forget that it was autumn in Tuscany, that in a few hours the light and warmth would be gone and the wind would come and work its way into your spine as you hurry home over the dark river.

You don't think about this when you're on a hill high above the old city of Florence, among parasol pines and cypress trees, on an October day that feels like June. From these heights, everything seems far away. Even the Duomo looks like a toy model.

A few hours earlier I had been down on one of the city's

ancient streets, head cocked to get a look at the slender cross on Dante's Church, when I was nearly clipped by a platoon of helmeted sightseers on Segways flying toward the Piazza della Signoria, where I later spotted them parked in front of the replica of the *David* as if it were the screen at a drive-in movie theater.

Autumn used to be off-season in Florence. Henry James wrote of his "brilliant" October days there, when the "musing wanderer" had the town to himself and "the native population itself seemed scanty." I was seeking some of that quietude—some *dolce far niente*, sweet idleness—in the early days of fall, the season of truffles and chestnuts, when people soak up the last warm hours in Adirondack chairs along the Arno, sipping wine at tables on the grass. Yet too often I found myself in an alley behind a band of tourists and a guide holding aloft a closed umbrella like a torch.

Fewer places are truly off-season nowadays. And besides, Florence hasn't historically been a place of peace. The streets around the Duomo used to have names like Death, Hell, and The Way of the Discontented, as Mary McCarthy writes in *The Stones of Florence*. At the Bargello, the Renaissance sculpture museum, people were executed. "In the lovely Piazza della Signoria," as an itinerary card from my hotel described it, men were hanged, and the preacher Girolamo Savonarola was burned, like the cosmetics and books he denounced in the bonfires of the vanities. During the building of the Duomo, "from dawn to dusk the air rang with the blows of the blacksmith's hammer and with the rumble of oxcarts and the shouting of orders," as Ross King tells us in *Brunelleschi's Dome,* his account of the colossal dome and its creator, Filippo Brunelleschi. (Brunelleschi himself isn't getting much peace: I found his tomb behind bars, through an opening in a wall in the crowded gift shop of the Florence cathedral.)

Before I climbed the hill, I'd been planning to spend a quiet day in the heart of the old city. But then I was nearly mowed down at Dante's Church. At the Bargello, Michelangelo's *Bacchus* was surrounded by museumgoers. Across the street at the Church of Santa Maria Assunta of the Badia Fiorentina, a tour group had formed a blockade across the stairs. And so I crossed the Santa Trinita bridge—rebuilt several times since the thirteenth century after being destroyed by floods and being blown up by German troops at the end of World War II—to commune with Autumn, one of four statues, first installed in the seventeenth century, that represent the seasons and stand guard at the corners of the bridge.

Yet beneath Autumn's bare feet, teenagers were walking every which way, cyclists frantically rang their bells, and Vespas and motorcycles whizzed by within inches of my toes. Almost all walkers in this town are "in danger of death," as McCarthy noted. "If you step backward onto the pavement to look up at a palace, you will probably be run over."

I fled back across the bridge, past the men holding selfie sticks like fishing rods, asking "Selfie?" as you went by. I hurried past Primavera, the statue of Spring who lost her head after the German bombing. When the bridge was reopened in the 1950s, the statues of the seasons, including the headless Primavera, were returned to their posts. The Parker Pen Company offered $3,000 to anyone who could locate the head, according to the art historian Eve Borsook, though it wasn't until 1961 that a dredging crew found it in the Arno. After a brief display on a red velvet cushion in the Palazzo Vecchio, Borsook wrote, "it was firmly replaced on the shoulders of La Primavera." No one today would know her history but for the faint crack, like a necklace, surrounding her pale throat.

I turned onto Lungarno degli Acciaiuoli, a busy road along the Arno, on my way to the Florence National Central Library, where I bounded up the stairs. At last: quiet.

"No visitors," said the woman behind the glass.

Visits, as I would have known had I checked in advance, were by appointment only.

Appointments are not necessary to get into the Biblioteca Medicea Laurenziana near the Piazza San Lorenzo, the library that houses works collected by the era's leading humanists, but it, too, swells with visitors eager to see its unusual entrance hall staircase with elliptical steps designed by Michelangelo.

Yet there was another place touched by Michelangelo that I suspected could offer some peace, one that I was certain wouldn't require a reservation: the Porte Sante cemetery.

The cemetery is on a hill above the old city, behind the Basilica of San Miniato, named for a third-century Christian martyr known as Saint Miniatus. Accused of being a heretic, Miniatus was beheaded, after which he is said to have picked up his decapitated head and walked from the Arno up into the hills to his hermitage. This is no easy task, even with one's head intact.

My walk from the old city began by crossing the Arno, where for centuries wool was washed, hides submerged, and marble floated from Carrera. On the Oltrarno, I passed under

Porta di San Miniato, the old stone arch at the base of a hill, and went up Via del Monte alle Croci toward terraced steps that grew steeper and steeper, along a row of trees. What at first appeared to be a few thin trunks here and there turned out to be tall, plain crosses planted in the dirt. Chickens pecked the ground around them, their red combs twitching.

As you ascend the steps, the narrow, gray streets give way to the dark green, velvet hillside, dotted with farmhouses the color of mustard, and stone fortifications designed by Michelangelo to protect Florence during the siege of 1529. When the stairs eventually end, you step up onto a curving sidewalk beneath tree boughs and street lamps, as black and slender as calligraphy. There are benches from which to take in the sweeping views of the city and the blue mountains that envelop it. You are, however, not quite at the basilica.

San Miniato is perched on the hill on the opposite side of the road. I dashed across to avoid being hit by the cars that whip around the curve, climbing more stone steps, past balustrades, between manicured hedges and through rusted gates, to the top. Yet before going around back to the adjoining cemetery, I went inside the basilica, down into the candlelit crypt, where tourists were chatting beside a sign asking for silence. Florence is filled with *"Silenzio!"* signs, including an electric one in the Basilica of Santa Croce with the illuminated words SILENCE—RESPECT. That this needs to be spelled out in all caps and lit up like a sign for a twenty-four-hour diner in a basilica completed in the fourteenth century is an indication of what one is occasionally up against.

Michelangelo is among the luminaries buried in Santa

Croce. In life, he spent a good deal of time alone. Because he could withdraw comfortably into solitude, some people considered him arrogant; others thought he was bizarre, Ascanio Condivi, a fellow Florentine painter and his biographer, tells us. But he believed Michelangelo was neither. While his work made him solitary, Condivi said it "afforded him such delight and fulfillment that the company of others not only failed to satisfy him but even distressed him, as if it distracted him from his meditation."

Michelangelo often worked late, sometimes illuminating his workspace by attaching a candle to his hat. When sculpting the *David,* he had a wooden framework built around the marble slab so he could labor unseen.

"No one should think it strange that Michelangelo loved solitude, for he was deeply in love with his art," wrote the artist Giorgio Vasari in *The Lives of the Artists,* his wide-ranging account of the work of his friends and contemporaries, who also happened to include the likes of Brunelleschi, da Vinci, and Donatello. Both Vasari and Condivi tell us that it was not surprising but rather, necessary, that Michelangelo avoided companionship. "Anyone who wants to devote himself to the study of art must shun the society of others," Vasari said. "In fact, a man who gives his time to the problems of art is never alone."

When a friend told Michelangelo that it was a shame that he wasn't married, with sons who could inherit his works, Michelangelo replied, "I've always had only too harassing a wife in this demanding art of mine, and the works I leave behind will be my sons." Creators and innovators, regardless of gender or sexual orientation, have long wrestled with the balance of work and relationships. Remember Darwin? Then there's Keats, who told his brother and sister-in-law that he never wanted to marry, insisting, "My Happiness would not be so fine, as my Solitude is sublime," though he did get engaged. Amelia Earhart was of like mind, writing to her future husband: "You must know again my reluctance to marry, my feeling that I shatter thereby chances in work which means most to me."

Like Santa Croce, San Miniato is a popular destination, not only for what's inside the basilica but also for the panoramic vistas of Florence below. Visitors seem to spend as much if not more time photographing the city as exploring the basilica or the old graves on either side of its facade, some brightened with roses or strewn with candy. Fewer still go around back, up the hill, to the sprawling Porte Sante cemetery behind the bell tower, which Michelangelo lined with bales of wool and mattresses to protect from cannonballs during the siege. There, on a wooden bench in the sun or a shaded path between mausoleums, you can be alone among lovers sculpted in marble, winged angels that never take flight, and bronze busts of men turning green with age, casting shadows in the afternoon light.

Some mausoleums are ornate, with colored marble and onion domes. Others are plain. One of the latter almost resembles a child's drawing of a house, with a peaked roof and the number 37 on its stone face, the color of oysters. It sits along a stone and moss path near other drab crypts in a kind of condo development for the departed. When I arrived, its gates were wound with chains, and its curtains were closed. I would have breezed right by were it not for a white card dangling from a red ribbon tied to the gate. I flipped it over and saw a familiar face.

Frankly, I thought there would be more cards—and flowers, too; maybe even toys. But there was just the card with a couple of holes punched in the corner for the red ribbon to slip through. The paper looked as if it had been faded by rain and bleached by sun. On it was a drawing of a boy with a long nose wearing a cone hat. Above him were two words so faint, it was as if they had been written by a ghost: "Padre Pinocchio."

The mausoleum is said to contain the remains of Carlo Collodi, a Florentine and the author of *Pinocchio*, though if you go looking for his resting place by that name, as I initially did, you won't find him. He was born Carlo Lorenzini and is buried in the family mausoleum, where above the gates is the family name: LORENZINI.

I was still holding the drawing when I heard voices approaching. I left and took a narrow path between mausoleums, across short, patchy grass, past empty planters black with grime, to tombs overlooking the Duomo. From this distance its burnt-orange bricks were the color of dying leaves. While it was being built, inhabitants of the area were evicted from their homes, and "the bones of long-dead Florentines were exhumed from their graves" to create a piazza beside the church, King tells us. It's fitting, then, that some of the most striking views of the Duomo can be had while standing amid vaults and headstones.

By now, the sun was going down. There's probably an hour at which being alone in an old cemetery goes from serene to spooky, but I didn't care to find out precisely when it was. I took a final walk around before following a path out, past a church bulletin board, where hanging from a string on a yellow push-pin was a palm-sized Pinocchio, one tiny wooden arm raised as if waving hello.

Or was it goodbye?

———

Something about the sign didn't look right.

Once again I had strayed from the heart of the old city, walking north toward the Rifredi railway station. I was on an ordinary street with what, at first blush, appeared to be an ordinary No Entry sign. But it was not, it turns out, so ordinary.

Your run-of-the-mill Florentine No Entry sign is a red circle with a floating white bar. This one, upon closer inspection, had a stick figure, like the ones on construction work signs, hovering behind the white bar. In one of its tiny hands was a chisel, which it was using to sculpt the white bar as if it were a slab of marble. In the "marble" I could make out traces of a face: an eye, a nose, a mouth. The stick figure was carving a statue from the white slab, just as Michelangelo had sculpted the *David*. I couldn't help but smile at this bit of whimsy: a wink to those who looked close enough to see it.

But that wasn't all. Nearby, the vertical white arrow of a One Way sign had also been reimagined. On top of the arrow point, someone had added a white circle signifying a head. And above the circle was a halo—so that the skyward-pointing arrow resembled an angel in a white robe.

On a yellow-and-black construction sign, a stick figure worker now had a ball and chain shackled to his ankle. A few blocks away, a red and blue No Parking sign was partly covered in black webbing that looked as if it had been shot there by Spider-Man.

On a directional sign, the horizontal arrow had been altered so that it dissolved into daisies.

These doctored street signs were as plentiful as wildflowers. I found them on the way out of the old city, near the Piazza della Indipendenza, where people relaxed on benches in their fall coats. I found them along twisted gnarls of railroad tracks and on the other side of a low, graffitied tunnel on the way to the hills of Montughi, to the Robert Baden Powell garden, and to the Frederick Stibbert Museum. The Stibbert is the opulent former home of a nineteenth-century financier and his collection of armory from the fifteenth through nineteenth centuries, which features a cavalcade hall with rows of horses and statues of men in armor.

But I was more interested in a man named Clet Abraham, the French street artist who lives in Florence and cleverly uses stickers to turn arrows into angels and No Entry sign bars into sculptures. It's hardly the sort of art you expect to seek out in a city of Renaissance masterpieces. But then, all those masterpieces can wear you out.

Stendhal, the nineteenth-century author of *The Red and the Black*, reportedly saw so much breathtaking art in Florence that he felt faint. He isn't alone. Faintness—not to mention sweating, depression or euphoria, or having hallucinations—has been so common among tourists in Florence that when Graziella Magherini was the chief of psychiatry at the city's Santa Maria Nuova Hospital, she dubbed it the "Stendhal Syndrome."

"The Stendhal Syndrome occurs most frequently in Florence, because we have the greatest concentration of Renaissance art in the world," Magherini once told *Metropolis M* magazine. "People seldom see just a single work, but overload themselves with hundreds of masterpieces in a short period."

The condition is controversial; it doesn't appear in the American Psychiatric Association's *Diagnostic and Statistical Manual of Mental Disorders*. But afflicted or not, spying a Clet Abraham on the street after a day of sightseeing is like being served a cool limoncello. Although his works were throughout the city, few people seemed to notice them. Indeed, many of the objects and talismans I've "found" while traveling—the mystery book in the garden in Paris, euro coins, hacked road signs—were not actually hidden. They were there in plain sight, waiting to be seen. To borrow a phrase from the poet Gary Snyder, solitude endows us with a kind of "power-vision" that heightens the senses and raises alertness to everyday things that can be all too easy to overlook.

As tour groups streamed by, I went Easter egg hunting for more of Abraham's signs. Whenever I found one, I stopped to admire it while people pushed past me, as if neither I nor the sign were there. It was like being in a museum and having the artworks to myself. And in this unexpected way, on street corners and under lamplights, I found a kind of solitude despite the throngs.

Scouting for signs reminded me of the game that was a regular feature in the magazine *Highlights for Children,* in which you had to search for objects hidden among illustrations of everyday scenes; of looking for the name "Nina" disguised within Al Hirschfeld's caricatures in the Sunday *New York Times;* of a "found things" grade-school homework assignment that required each of us to go off with a grown-up to hunt down objets trouvés on the streets. These sorts of quests take on new meaning as an adult. You can make up your own games (like tracking down Parisian sphinxes or Clet Abraham signs) or project, like the photographer Stefan Draschan's series "People Sleeping in Museums," featuring visitors catnapping amid artworks. Or pick up something like the "Anywhere Travel Guide," a deck of seventy-five cards, each containing an instruction, like "Start walking until you see something particularly yellow. Notice this something," or "If you can see a shop from where you are, step inside it. Ask someone there where to go next."

One Anywhere card directs you to follow a stranger. This, it so happens, is something da Vinci used to do. He was in the habit of spending entire days following men and women he considered to be striking, particularly anyone with a "strange head of hair or beard," according to Vasari. Later, da Vinci would draw the person from memory.

In 1969, the performance artist Vito Acconci trailed strangers on foot around New York City for as long as the person remained in a public space. (While it sounds supremely creepy, it's considered one of Acconci's most notable works.) Each day for about a month, Acconci chose someone and followed him or her through the streets of New York, exploring ideas about public and private space, chronicling his wanderings with notes and photos. The "following" ended when the person went into a private space.

In the 1980s, the French conceptual artist Sophie Calle surreptitiously followed and photographed strangers on the streets of Paris simply for the pleasure of it. At one point at a gathering she met a man whom she had followed earlier in the day. "During the course of our conversation, he told me he was planning an imminent trip to Venice," she wrote in her book *Suite Vénitienne*. "I decided to follow him." She then hopped a train to Italy, where, disguised in a blond wig, she dined alone, followed and photographed the unsuspecting man (known in the book as Henri B.), and kept time-stamped notes about his movements through Venice. She got careless—or allowed herself to become careless—and was eventually discovered. But Henri B. was a good sport about it, and was apparently more flattered than fearful. Calle tried to photograph him during their meeting but he raised a hand to hide his face. He had his own rules.

Acconci (whose Twitter biography once read "Vito Acconci is now following you on Twitter") described himself as "a situation maker." Alone, you can be one, too, designing your own game. With its carnival atmosphere—the carousels and hidden passageways; the costume helmets and armor you can try on at the Stibbert Museum; the sculptures and fountains you slip coins into for good luck—Florence lends itself to this sort of playfulness.

———

That evening, I returned to the Savoy. A boutique hotel in a grand old building that dates to the 1890s, it had pale rooms with high ceilings, parquet floors, and large windows that looked onto the Duomo or the Piazza della Repubblica, the square that was once the site of the Roman forum and the Jewish ghetto. It was also the backdrop to Ruth Orkin's 1951 photo of a solo woman traveler, *American Girl in Italy,* which would appear in *Cosmopolitan* magazine with a feature titled "Don't Be Afraid to Travel Alone." The Savoy has since undergone extensive renovations but at the time, my room was an elegantly spare retreat. I padded barefoot across the smooth wood herringbone floor to the wide window and let in the hum of the piazza below. The evening pantomime was under way: young people standing in small circles, smoking, talking about some intrigue or other, filing in and out of a restaurant serving pizza and wine. This is the beauty of old European buildings; they're high enough to have crow's nests but not so high that you're isolated from the rhythms of the street. I leaned out. On one side of the piazza was Gilli, a café and pastry shop that's been in Florence in one spot or another since 1733; at the far side of the piazza was an Apple store. I left the window open and took my laptop into bed to write.

Within the hour my eyes were fluttering closed. I got up and returned to the window. The piazza was still full as I reached for the shutters. The bit of effort required to swing them open and closed marked the beginning and end of each day with casual ceremony. It was far more satisfying than brushing aside a curtain or tugging a cord. To throw open the shutters was to invite in the morning. To close them with a soft thud was to acknowledge the passing of another day.

I pulled them toward my chest, lifted one silver latch and then the other, and quieted the city.

# Alone with Venus

*On Seeing*

*I spent three hours this morning principally in the contem-*
*plation of the Niobe, and of a favourite Apollo; all worldly*
*thoughts and cares seem to vanish . . .*
    —Percy Bysshe Shelley in a letter to Mrs. Shelley from
      Florence, 1821

No one was standing in front of *The Birth of Venus*. It was just
me and the goddess with the auburn hair.

I had shuffled through the Uffizi Gallery's metal detectors
with the Saturday morning crowd, walked up the staircase,
through the corridors with the painted ceilings, into a room of
Botticellis—and not a soul was there. On the wall, as if hanging
over someone's living room couch, was Botticelli's fifteenth-
century masterwork: the goddess of love in a scallop shell, just
off the shores of Cyprus. It was the very image so often slapped
on anything that can be sold in a museum bookshop—T-shirts,
tote bags, calendars, keychains—not to mention featured on
the national side of the Italian ten euro cent. Despite the fame

of one of his best-known works, Botticelli is said to have been so poor in his old age that he would have died of hunger had not deep-pocketed friends like Lorenzo de' Medici come to his aid. I approached the painting cautiously, concerned, as usual, that I had strayed into some off-limits area. But no alarms sounded, and no one rushed in to warn me away. I was alone with one of the most famous women in the world.

I wish I could say, as I stood at Venus's feet that morning, that I allowed eye and mind to wander slowly over the ripples of the blue-green sea she floated in on, the pink roses tumbling in the wind, her long strands of hair, the folds of the cloak about to be draped around her naked shoulders. Yet instead—I put my iPhone between us and began taking photos.

It is rare, seemingly impossible really, to have the opportunity to view a masterpiece under such conditions. You generally can't so much as glance at Venus, or the *Mona Lisa*, without also seeing the back of someone's head or hearing an audio tour spilling from a stranger's headset. I wasn't in some small museum, like the Horne. The Uffizi is notorious for its long lines, congested galleries, and pickpockets. And there I was, alone with Venus, taking photo after photo like some paparazzo. But by the time I realized what I was doing it was too late—footsteps sounded in the hall. I'd been given the gift of privacy, *silenzio*, in one of the most magnificent and unlikely places. And I squandered it.

What had I been trying to achieve? Susan Sontag wrote that photographs are a way of imprisoning reality, of making it "an exotic prize to be tracked down and captured by the diligent hunter-with-a-camera."

Sometimes, the hunter is clumsy. In 2017, when a woman visiting an exhibition at Factory in Los Angeles tried to take a selfie, she fell onto an installation and ruined $200,000 worth of art. (Many people have also been injured, some fatally, while absorbed in getting the perfect shot. In 2016, researchers found that 127 people had died while trying to take selfies since March 2014.) Yet even in 1977, before the Instagram age, Sontag observed that the camera was a crutch for the traveler, one that made having an experience "identical with taking a photograph of it."

By trying to keep the moment forever, I'd denied myself the immediacy of the experience of the painting as well as the quiet gallery. And, as I would later learn, that's the sort of thing that may affect not only the moment, but the memory of the moment, too. Linda A. Henkel, a psychology professor at Fairfield University in Connecticut, calls this the "photo-taking impairment effect." In her experiments, participants took a guided tour of a museum that housed paintings, sculptures, pottery, tools, jewels, and mosaics. The participants were told to simply observe some objects and to photograph others. Henkel's findings, published in *Psychological Science,* revealed that photographing the objects in their entirety diminished people's memory of them. Participants who did so, as opposed to just observing the work, remembered fewer objects and fewer details about those objects. They relied on the camera, Henkel said, "to 'remember' for them."

There was, however, an exception to this finding. When participants zoomed in to photograph a particular part of an object, such as a statue's feet or a painting's sky, its memory was retained. The extra attention and thought involved in focusing and zooming in on part of the object seemed to eliminate the impairment effect.

Studies that explore how photo-taking does or doesn't affect memory have had seemingly conflicting results. Subsequent research published in 2017 in *Psychological Science* found that taking photos aided visual memory but hurt auditory memory. After conducting four studies, professors at New York University's Stern School of Business, USC's Marshall School of Business, the Wharton School of the University of Pennsylvania, and the Yale School of Management concluded that "even when people don't take a photo of a particular object, like a sculpture, but have a camera with them and the intention to take photos, they remember that sculpture better than people who did not have a camera with them."

Whatever the latest research finds, few of us are going to stop taking photos, even those who are uninterested in posting minute-by-minute accounts of our trips on social media. There is pleasure in the process, in composing a shot, of seeing differently. "When I'm on my own with my camera . . . it feels as if I am in a room of my own, a self-contained world," Patti Smith said in an interview for *Camera Solo,* the catalogue that accompanied an exhibition of her photographs at the Wadsworth Atheneum Museum of Art in Hartford, Connecticut. On the road, I like photographing fellow solitary travelers. There's something joyful in the woman sitting on a wall along the Arno, scribbling in a notebook; the man lying on his stomach on a bench with a book in the garden of the Rodin Museum in Paris; the woman sunbathing beside the Seine.

Yet for many of us, our cameras are also our phones. And that's where we may run into trouble, because a smartphone can so easily undermine savoring. "If you are doing this," as Fran Lebowitz said while making texting motions with her thumbs in the Martin Scorsese documentary *Public Speaking,* "*that's* where you are."

According to one study, the average adult checks his or her phone thirty times a day, while the average millennial checks his or her phone more than 150 times a day. I can barely stand to keep my phone in a bag on my shoulder. I might want to get directions, find a coffee shop, listen to a podcast, or answer my editor's texts. Admittedly, I sometimes use my phone to make notes while walking, joining the ranks of the so-called smart-phone zombies.

Little wonder that people around the world are taking Internet Sabbaths, turning off their devices to return to themselves. In the United States, Reboot, a group inspired by Jewish traditions, organizes a phone-free "National Day of Unplugging." Hotels as varied as the Renaissance Pittsburgh and the Mandarin Oriental have at one point or another offered "digital detox vacations" that encouraged guests to hand over their smartphones. Intrepid Travel, a group tour company with headquarters in Melbourne, Australia, has offered digital detox tours—"exclusive departures where there'll be no social media and no cellphones. For real"—to places like Morocco and India. Forever Resorts, which offers rental houseboats at lakes and national parks across the United States, featured an "unplugging ceremony" during which guests gathered around a lockbox to impound their mobile phones. Marriott and Renaissance

Caribbean & Mexico Resorts rolled out "Braincation," tech-free zones at nine properties across the Caribbean and Mexico.

In 2017, an entire country took action when France introduced a "right to disconnect" law that gives workers the legal right to ignore work emails when they are not on the clock. Texts, messages, and emails "colonize the life of the individual to the point where he or she eventually breaks down," as Benoît Hamon, a former French education minister, stated.

Even some of the designers of the technology are turning off notifications on their smartphones and using Internet and app blockers like Freedom to reclaim their time (more on that in the Tips and Tools section of this book). For example, Tristan Harris, a former design ethicist at Google, created the Center for Humane Technology, which advocates for and spurs the creation of technology that's not distracting and addictive.

As my iPhone and I were entering the crimson Room of Michelangelo and the Florentine Painters, a family was just leaving. I found myself alone again, this time with a statue of a reclining Cleopatra and with the Holy Family in the vibrant panel painting *Doni Tondo*. The Uffizi on that autumn morning seemed to exist only for me. A guard was seated on a chair, head leaning back against the wall, snoring as I walked across the gilded neoclassical room ringed with marble statues that tell the story of the myth of Niobe, a noblewoman who boasted that she had more children than Leto, the mother of Apollo and Artemis. (Things didn't go well for Niobe after that; her many sons and daughters were killed.)

On the Uffizi's rooftop terrace, where visitors can look out over the city and the battlements of the Palazzo Vecchio, there were only two people, and they were sitting on a bench in silence. It's one thing to occasionally find yourself alone in, say, the Bargello in the majolica room, even in the Mary Magdalene Chapel with the crucifix attributed to Michelangelo. Or, after waiting for tour groups to pass, inside the silent Badia Fiorentina. But that morning in the Uffizi was extraordinary.

No one was in front of the Bronzinos. In a nearby room, I walked right up to da Vinci's *Annunciation* and *Baptism of Christ*. Next, I was face-to-face with Medusa, the Caravaggio parade shield that inspired Vik Muniz's *Medusa Marinara,* 1999. The shield was decorated with her severed head, mouth agape, writhing serpents for hair, blood spurting from her neck. Now *this* was a formidable Medusa.

There was more blood and gore nearby at Artemisia Gentileschi's *Judith Slaying Holofernes,* and another Caravaggio, *The Sacrifice of Isaac.* It was a bit much for a Saturday morning. I preferred the romance of another Venus—Titian's *Venus of Urbino,* a voluptuous nude reclining on a white-sheeted divan, a hand lazily resting on the V between her legs.

We, too, were alone. For as long I dared to stare at her, she stared back, "unashamed," as the text beside the painting said, with her luminous nudity, the white curve of her belly; herself.

# KNOWLEDGE

# The Secret Corridor

*Schooling Yourself*

*You can have no dominion greater or less than that over yourself.*

—Leonardo da Vinci, *The Notebooks of Leonardo da Vinci*

One end of the corridor begins behind locked doors in the walls of the Uffizi, zags across the Ponte Vecchio and over the Arno, through the top of the Santa Felicita church, and into the Pitti Palace, about half a mile away. It was built in the 1500s for Francesco I de' Medici and Joanna of Austria, which enabled the Medici to walk in privacy and safety between their offices in the Uffizi and their palace in the Boboli Gardens. (Safety was a legitimate concern: In 1478, members of the Pazzi family conspired to end the Medici rule by killing the brothers Lorenzo and Giuliano during Mass, according to Machiavelli's account; Giuliano did not survive.)

The outline of the corridor, with its small, caged windows, can be seen from the Ponte Vecchio, above the little ocher shops that cling to it like barnacles. From its windows you can watch tourists on the old bridge, shopping for gloves and gold, unaware of your eyes on them as they take selfies along the Arno. This is fitting: The walls of the hidden corridor are lined with self-portraits from the Uffizi's collection, some of the oldest in the world.

The corridor is named for its creator, Giorgio Vasari, who is hardly a household name even though he designed, or helped design, some of the most iconic churches and palaces in Florence. Nearly every book about Renaissance art, or block of wall text in a museum in Florence, includes his name. "Vasari tells us the story," begins the text beside Donatello's tomb. "A fact mentioned by Vasari," reads a sign at the Bargello about the discovery of a portrait of Dante by Giotto. "According to Vasari," says another in the Reading Room at the Biblioteca Medicea Laurenziana. The city is so filled with references to Vasari that, as with sphinxes in Paris, a traveler can make a game of counting the number of times his name is encountered in the course of a day.

The ubiquity of Vasari's name is largely due to his having written *The Lives of the Artists*, the source of much (occasionally embellished and inadvertently incorrect) art history of the period. Were blogs around in his time, Vasari would have been the must-read insider, posting about jealousies (such as Donatello's annoyance at Brunelleschi's criticism of his carving of a Christ) and rivalries (da Vinci versus Michelangelo!) of his age. He would have had regular posts about Botticelli's pranks (Botticelli once altered a painting to fool an apprentice into thinking he was seeing things that weren't there) and an exclusive about an incident in which the goldsmith Francesco

Francia was shown a statue of Julius by Michelangelo and proceeded to compliment its bronze casting rather than its crafts-
manship. Michelangelo quipped: "I owe as much to Pope Julius
who gave me the bronze as you owe to the chemists who give
you your colors for painting." Michelangelo concluded, Vasari
tells us, by calling Francia a fool.

Vasari's own work can be seen in Florence's most popular
sites. He had a hand in details of the Santa Croce, Santa Maria
Novella, San Lorenzo, and Ognissanti churches. He worked on
grottoes for the Boboli Gardens, helped complete the Biblioteca
Medicea Laurenziana, and designed Michelangelo's tomb, as
well as a little building known as the Uffizi.

In 1966, during one of the worst floods in the history of Florence, hundreds of Renaissance masterworks and library collec-
tions were submerged. Vasari's *The Last Supper* was underwater
for more than twelve hours and took half a century to finally be
restored and reinstalled in Santa Croce. Paula Deitz, the editor
of the *Hudson Review,* called it "the main event" of the city's 2016
anniversary commemorations. She had been in Florence during the flood with her future husband, the editor and poet Frederick Morgan, and wrote fifty years later that Vasari's five-panel
painting was "the final, most complex, severely damaged masterpiece in the flood to be restored."

This history, these stories, were among the things I read
about in the sweet anticipatory hours before my trip, and in the
months that came after. I looked at maps, photos, and paintings
by Raphael, Caravaggio, and Botticelli, who, I learned, painted
other versions of his auburn-haired Venus in which she was
alone, unaccompanied by winds or Graces. I read in Horace

Walpole's letter about coining the word "serendipity" that he had received a portrait of the Grand Duchess Bianca Capello—painted by Vasari. And, of course, I read Vasari. I read Machiavelli, Dante, and da Vinci, too, giving myself the art history class I always wished I'd taken.

Da Vinci himself was mostly self-taught. Just skim his notebooks and you'll see how he brought a spirit of investigation and cross-pollination into everyday life, in observations and instructions about painting, geography, zoology, anatomy, and astronomy. (His notebooks are available for free online, including at Gutenberg.org, and can be used as a model for creating your own notebooks about whatever topics interest you.)

In addition to thoughts about when and where to study, and how to practice and learn, da Vinci wrote notes to himself about a startling variety of subjects he wanted to understand: "Learn to work flesh colours in tempera," said one. "Learn levelling and how much soil a man can dig out in a day," said another. Perhaps his way of thinking is best summed up by one of the notebook headings: "How something may be learnt everywhere."

While a certain amount of our happiness is genetically predetermined, some measure of it is within our control, and one of the things we can do to maximize the latter, Sorja Lyubomirsky has found, is to "learn until the day you die."

Learning new things goes hand in hand with what positive psychologists call engagement, an element of well-being that can ultimately lead to what the psychologist Mihaly Csikszentmihalyi called "flow." Flow involves that sensation of total absorption in an activity like painting or playing music, the feeling that "clock time" has disappeared. You're in the zone and nothing else—sleep, food, body aches—can distract your focus. Csikszentmihalyi reached that conclusion after he and his colleagues spent years interviewing all sorts of creative people, including painters, scientists, and mountain climbers. Beethoven's circle had their own word for the composer's experience of flow: "raptus." In his biography of the composer, Jan Swafford describes raptus as a withdrawal into a profound trance. "Alone in rooms, alone in nature, alone in his raptus, Beethoven was happiest and always would be."

Learning is part of the joy of travel. Learning about the Vasari corridor, for instance, was easy and affordable. Actually gaining admission to the Vasari corridor was less so. You couldn't just show up and go at your own pace; you had to be part of a tour. The Uffizi offered a limited number of tickets (not included in the price of museum admission), but even weeks before my trip, the tours were sold out. And so I ended up buying a $75 ticket through Viator.com, which offered tours by local guides throughout the world. (Note: The process of visiting the Vasari corridor, even the art on display inside, may be changing. The director of the Uffizi proposed renovating the corridor, opening it to more visitors, and moving some of its paintings elsewhere. The Uffizi is undergoing renovations in other areas, too—it has already reorganized its Botticelli rooms—to help alleviate overcrowding. And easier online booking directly through the museum is up and running.)

My tour group was instructed to meet on a side street outside the Uffizi. Most of us had gathered early and signed in with clipboard-carrying organizers. Half of us would go into the corridor first, and the other half would follow. We were standing in the street, waiting to begin, when a few women arrived and told one of the organizers that one member of their party was running late. Could the rest of us wait? they asked. For reasons that were unclear, the organizer then asked us all if anyone traveling alone would be willing to volunteer to join the group that would depart later.

I was scheduled to meet John, a friend and fellow *flâneur* who was working for the *New York Times* in London, for lunch immediately after the tour in a nearby piazza.

Before I ever traveled alone, I traveled with John. He was my solo travel training wheels. After all, we aren't necessarily born good travelers; we learn to be them. And John was being one with savoir vivre, traveling alone extensively for work and pleasure, all the while using points and miles to get upgraded to business class, and into airport lounges and better hotels. We first met at the *Times,* before he became the editor of a travel-themed section called "Escapes."

When you're alone, John said, there's no performance anxiety about making everyone in the group happy. For instance, while in Osaka, he decided to eat at a *katsu* counter instead of waiting for a table—something he would not have done if he were entertaining others. Alone, he could make last-minute decisions about how to spend an afternoon, or simply abandon a museum if the exhibition didn't grab him. "The defining word," he said, "is 'freedom.'"

In the case of the Vasari corridor tour, I didn't have the freedom of time. The tour was already running late, which would mean that if I offered to switch groups, I would keep John waiting in a piazza even longer than he already would have to be.

Being requested to switch seats or groups is familiar ground for solo travelers. There are all kinds of reasons travelers, solo or not, desire certain seats. We may have a tight connection, so a place near the exit is crucial. We may have a business meeting and know a particular seat will give us a better chance at some shut-eye. We may be anxious fliers and find one spot less stressful than another. We may have mental or physical limitations; not all disabilities are visible. Maybe we just like looking out the window. For some travelers, the view from 35,000 feet is one of life's great romantic pleasures, and a treasured part of a once-a-year vacation.

Most people want to be helpful. A survey about airline etiquette from Travel Leaders Group, one of the largest traditional travel agencies in the United States, asked travelers: "If you were flying alone and a couple or family asked you to switch seats so that they could sit together, what would you do?" Most said they would move. Whether they actually would do so is another matter—people's good intentions do not necessarily match up with their actions—but let's take them at their word. The second most popular answer was that they would move— but only if the new seat wasn't a middle seat.

Finding no willing volunteers, the tour organizer announced it was time to go.

We were led to a hallway in the Uffizi in front of two tall wooden doors with red push-bars and a box that suggested

that they were an emergency exit. Most visitors, myself included, would have wandered right by them. A man in a suit
and tie stood in front of the doors while our guide, a professor,
handed out listening devices. After some fiddling with wires
and some more standing around and waiting, the man in the
suit began to unlock the doors. People raised their smartphones
to film the reveal as if we had just heard the opening bars of a
rock concert.

When the doors parted I could see beyond them a drab staircase leading down and a curved ceiling painted with imaginary
beasts. I adjusted the volume on the device in my ear. A guard
motioned in our direction, and we moved forward into the
mouth of the tunnel, inside the walls of the Uffizi, the doors
closing behind us.

"Stay in the center," warned a guard.

If someone moved a little too close to a portrait or lingered
too long in one spot, she would snap at him or her in Italian,
uncrossing her arms just long enough to wave them, lending
the tour the air of a fifth-grade class trip. When the guard
wasn't doing either of these things, she was tapping the screen
of her smartphone or hugging herself as if she had a perpet-
ual chill.

The halls were lined with gold frames. Hundreds of eyes
watched from the walls, from portraits by Andrea del Sarto,
Giovanni Domenico Ferretti, Marc Chagall, and women artists
absent from the main halls of the Uffizi. Here: Thérèse Schwar-
tze. There: Rosalba Carriera.

Now and then the guard looked up from her phone long
enough to remind us to keep moving along. Another tour

group was behind us, and one a few feet ahead. We were like floats in a parade, each with its own watchful minder. We followed the professor—who had the thick curls of Michelangelo's *David*, and was wearing jeans, a blazer, and a knotted scarf with fringe at its end—across the Ponte Vecchio. Round, caged windows offered postcard views of the Arno, the city's terracotta roofs and old yellow buildings with pale blue shutters.

After the corridor crosses over the river it runs through the top of the church of Santa Felicita, where a private box opposite the altar allowed the Medicis to attend Mass high above the worshippers.

If you were lucky, and if your guard was feeling charitable, at the end of the corridor you might get the nod to ascend a flight of steps and spend a few minutes—no more—in a secret room. Incredibly, our guard allowed us to do so.

The sound of our shoes on the steps echoed through the halls. The room itself was small, white, and lined with self-portraits that could have a place in a modern art museum. To the right was *Self Portrait—Submerged, 2013* by the video artist Bill Viola, who was underwater, wearing a blue button-front shirt, his skin seemingly moving as the water rocked across his body. On the opposite wall, along with works by Vanessa Beecroft and Yayoi Kusama, was the artist Jenny Holzer's 1981 "self-portrait" in words. Block letters on a square white background said:

**SOME DAYS YOU WAKE AND
IMMEDIATELY START TO WORRY.
NOTHING IN PARTICULAR IS WRONG,**

## IT'S JUST THE SUSPICION THAT FORCES ARE ALIGNING QUIETLY AND THERE WILL BE TROUBLE.

No sooner had we filed into the room than the guard began ushering us out, past an installation of a man climbing a ladder to the ceiling. I hadn't had a chance to look at the other works before we were herded back toward the steps and down another flight of stairs somewhere within the walls of the Pitti Palace, through arched wooden doors that looked as if they had been designed for a Smurf's house, and then—*poof!*—into the Boboli Gardens, beside a high palace wall covered with vines and lemons. The sky was impossibly blue, like the Buddha in the window of rue de la Parcheminerie.

To my left was the otherworldly Buontalenti Grotto, pink and green, dripping with stalactites and stalagmites. The guide in my ear explained: "Those are rocks made of sponges." He then began describing the sculptures inside the grotto, including Giambologna's *Venus Emerging from the Bath*. Yet despite the grotto's strange beauty, I couldn't keep my eyes on the fountain, as something was happening in the sky.

I pulled the listening device from my ear. I had no idea what I was looking at. Colorful blobs were not merely floating but hovering above us, changing shape like liquid in a lava lamp. Perhaps I'd been in the Vasari corridor too long. Maybe it was Stendhal Syndrome. Someone said "balloons," and because no other explanation made sense, I decided that they were, in fact, balloons. I stood in the October sun, craning my neck, watching them disappear into the stratosphere, wondering what celebration they had left early.

When they rose too high to see, I returned the listening device to the professor and thanked him. If the tour was ultimately not as revelatory as I had hoped, I had had weeks of excitedly anticipating that it would be—and that, as Elizabeth Dunn would say, was joy already in the bank.

I set off to meet John for lunch, leaving the group behind as I followed a wide, curving path between lampposts, past palm trees, toward the Egyptian obelisk and the lemon house, where the citrus trees winter. Near an allée of cypresses, I stopped at a water fountain with a hidden delight in its copper bowl: two tiny sculptures of what appeared to be skulls, facing each other like chicks in a nest, water splashing and babbling between them.

I walked on toward the sound of running water, to the grotto of Adam and Eve. The couple looked beat: faces fallen, alabaster bodies splashed with grime. Their grotto was decorated with mosaics of scallops and pebbles shaped like anchors, ropes, and a trident. On its back walls moss sprouted from the gaping mouth of a wild-haired gargoyle.

In a small pool at Adam and Eve's feet, orange koi swam back and forth, reminding me of the fish in the black water of the Basilica Cistern in Istanbul. I stood watching them, listening contentedly to the sound of falling water, until once again I heard footsteps approaching. I turned to go, my canvas sneakers crunching the gravel path toward the gate and the hill that leads back to the center of town.

In the fall, at night, a cold wind flies through the streets. The Arno is black, and you're suddenly aware of just how low the walls are along the bridges. The wind goes through your jacket, into your bones, as you're walking back to your hotel after seeing Verdi's *La Traviata* at Saint Mark's English Church, or after a Bloody Mary at the bar in the St. Regis. You hear your footsteps echo on the cobblestones. So can anyone else in the dark.

You walk, unsure of whether your uneasiness is an intuition of actual danger, or if your mind is merely spooling some noir fantasy. Being on your own can easily become chiaroscuro, an interplay of light and darkness. One night you're walking alone, imagining being plunked on the head and dumped into the Arno along with fifteenth-century Dominican friars and Rauschenberg's early works. Another night, you walk carefree through shadows.

On my last evening in the city, I went walking with no particular destination in mind. People seemed restless, pinballing around the crooked, ill-lit streets in coats and scarves, looking for something to do. Here and there, under pools of eerie, unflattering light, tourists were trying to buy leather gloves before the shops closed. Students were carousing. Tipsy lovers were embracing on the Ponte Vecchio, gazing at the graceful strings of bridges under an almost full moon.

Near my hotel, on the sidewalk in front of La Rinascente, the department store that takes its name from the Italian word for "rebirth," a woman was being arrested for shoplifting. There can come a point during a solo trip, no matter how fabulous it may be, that the air is let out. The night feels long. The cobble-stone piazza, where you began the day at a sunny sidewalk table with eggs and truffles, loses its charm. The pretty boutiques don't manage to lift your spirits, even as you're buying something for someone you love back home.

A wise friend once told me that when you're blue, what you're experiencing is weather, not climate. And bad weather, he pointed out, is fleeting. I decided to wait out this particular stretch with a piglet named Porcellino, the bronze sculpture in the Piazza del Mercato Nuovo.

"Piglet" suggests that its subject is cute. It's not. The beast is as thin as a Labrador with a face as long as a goat's. And, technically, it's a boar. The hair on its hide is matted into a kind of fauxhawk from its spine to the top of its head. On either side of its mouth, from which water dribbles, splayed teeth curve upward like horns. Sculpted into the base around the boar's pointy hooves slither creatures of mud and water: snails, a crab, a frog, a snake, a salamander, a turtle.

At night, the boar has a sickly green glow, with the exception of its long snout, which has acquired a shine from people touching it for good luck, though the process of acquiring said luck is actually a little more complicated than that: After rubbing the snout, you must place a coin in the boar's wet mouth and then get it to fall through a grate there amid the running water.

This sounds easier than it is. For one thing, the boar is popular, often ringed by giddy onlookers. And because there's no formal queue, it's every wish-maker for himself. I seized my opening, pushed a coin into Porcellino's mouth, and waited.

It didn't drop.

I stuck my hand deeper into the pig's cool, wet mouth, my fingers probing beneath the water for the grate, doubtlessly covered in some ancient Florentine fungus. Of course, the more anxious you become while doing this, the less likely you are to be successful, but I wasn't about to slink away in defeat and jockey for a chance to try all over again. I fumbled around blindly, drenching the sleeve of my leather jacket, my eyes on the boar's mouth, until—*plop!*—the coin fell.

"Well done," said an onlooker in Italian.

At least that's what I wanted to believe she said, just as I wanted to believe that the coin landed wherever it was supposed to land to ensure whatever it was supposed to ensure. Months later, I read that the way to make a coin fall easily through the grate on Il Porcellino is to use a heavy coin. Perhaps you get what you pay for.

I headed back toward the Savoy, past bins of leather handbags and colorful Università Firenze hoodies being sold by sneakered men under electric lights. I passed a few Clet Abraham No Entry signs, including one picturing a stick figure smashing a guitar, rock star–style, over the white bar. I passed children in hooded jackets on horses on a carousel, its little bulbs like stars, the sole light in a black square.

My own jacket was still damp when I returned to the hotel room. I pulled off my boots, shuttered the windows, and climbed into bed.

The next morning, hours before my flight home, I woke up to a lovely soft chorus of church bells—lucky, after all.

I left the Savoy and crossed the Piazza della Repubblica for a final walk. The streets had been hosed down. The Piazza della Signoria was empty: No one was photographing Neptune, and the copy of Michelangelo's *David* was alone. The mountains were soft and blue in the distance.

I walked over to the Basilica of Santa Croce and the Pazzi Chapel, a spare, serene space, which sets it apart from so many others in the city. Designed by Brunelleschi for the Florentine banking family that tried to overthrow the Medici, the chapel has a blue cupola above the altar with a fresco of zodiac signs. Glazed terra-cotta medallions picture the Evangelists, including Saint Mark with a lion and Saint John with a black bird. But for the most part, the chapel is white and pale gray. An umbrella dome is unadorned. Mary McCarthy called it a "sabbath of stillness." And on that autumn day, it was.

The doors were open to the morning and to the courtyard beyond. All cities have their silent hours. Even, as it turns out, Florence.

I raised my iPhone to the vaulted ceiling to take a photo of the underside of the dome and as I waited in the soft light for the lens to focus, a bird shot out of nowhere and streaked across the chapel. For an instant I thought the ceiling had begun moving—that Saint John's black bird had come to life.

I was stunned frozen. In a matter of seconds the bird was gone, but it had awoken the memory of my lost morning with Venus. I slipped the phone into my bag and stood still, and in silence contemplated the fresco, my days in the city, and all that I had learned—about art, history, architecture—in the hours I had to myself.

That last morning, it was early enough to walk the Santa

Trinita bridge and encounter no one other than the selfie-stick man, who at this time of day was sitting in a patch of sunlight and didn't even bother trying to sell me a stick.

A kayak sliced across the Arno. I crossed the river from the figure of Primavera with the crack around her neck, over to Autumn, Giovanni Caccini's statue of a man holding bunches of plump grapes to the blue sky. But that's as far as I got. I had a plane to catch.

In a few hours I would be back in my own city. There would still be pumpkins and gourds on the stoops of the brownstones, though not for long. Soon there would be wreaths on the doors and evergreens twinkling in the windows. And one morning people would look out and see that first wondrous snow of the season, dusting the sidewalks of New York and making the autumnal days in Florence seem far away.

Before crossing the bridge back toward the Savoy I paused at the bare feet of a marble sculpture by Taddeo Landini. It was a man huddled into himself, clutching to his naked, white chest a scrap of cloth, looking as cold as the stone from which he was cut: Winter.

PART IV

Winter

New York

# HOME

# The City

*On Assignment*

*Objects which are usually the motives of our travels by land and by sea are often overlooked and neglected if they lie under our eye.*

—Pliny the Younger

I've lived in New York all my life, the last eighteen years in Manhattan—"The City," as those of us who spent at least part of our childhoods in suburbia called it. We didn't need to name it. There was only one.

There was only one Manhattan, just as there is only one Chrysler Building, one Apollo Theater, one Metropolitan Opera House. Manhattan is where Walt Whitman strolled the Battery. It's where Houdini escaped from a box in the East River; where Patti Smith still sings. Manhattan is the guy selling bananas on the corner; children playing hide-and-seek in an Egyptian temple beyond the sloping glass wall of the Metropolitan Museum of Art.

My first impressions of Manhattan were through a backseat window of the family car as we drove in from Long Island to see a play or musical. I would dress up. I wanted the people who lived in the city to think I lived there, too, with the lights, the yellow cabs, the buildings so tall I couldn't see their tops even when I pressed my forehead to the window as we drove toward the Queens-Midtown Tunnel after the show. In the dark I would nod off to the rhythm of the road, the soft swish of passing cars, and when I opened my eyes we were on our driveway beside the weeping cherry tree under the stars. The whole night might have been a dream. But then I would look down at my feet and see a *Playbill*.

Maybe it's not surprising, then, that my first job in the city was with Don Frantz, a theatrical producer who at the time was fresh off of working on *Beauty and the Beast* and *The Lion King*. I wasn't qualified to touch so much as a horn on a wildebeest, but then Don didn't hire me to work on Broadway. I was hired to assist with his labor of love: carving giant corn mazes—Amazing Maize Mazes—on family and living history farms where happy visitors get lost for sport. Not that I was qualified for that either, but the applicant pool was smaller.

And so my early years in Manhattan were marked not by commutes past the Art Deco buildings of Midtown, but occasional forays to cornfields in Iowa, Pennsylvania, and the Carolinas. When home, I was one of those young people in black helping backstage at benefits and readings—bringing Lauren Bacall an AIDS ribbon, escorting Chita Rivera to the wings—and taking advantage of a New York job perk: free, last-minute house seats to Broadway shows.

This is Manhattan: One night you're in an orchestra seat; another, you're on a stranger's stoop, eating a pint of ice cream. You can go around the corner for coffee and along the way pass a film crew shooting the next blockbuster, Anna Wintour, or any number of people hoofing it in styles you'll never see in the pages of *Vogue*. Each of us has our tribes. And to each the city speaks: You with the little apartment and the big dream; you who are lost, cocky, unsure, uptight, all-in; you with the pink hair and the sad eyes—"Welcome to Manhattan," as the green sign says. You can be whomever you want to be and still get invited to the party.

Friends from my first years in the city have since moved away, though our haunts remain in one form or another: Down the Hatch, the basement grunge bar with "Atomic" chicken wings, is still in Greenwich Village; Zum Schneider, the Bavarian beer garden, is still in Alphabet City; the Limelight is still in Chelsea, though it's no longer a nightclub in a Gothic Revival church—now it's a few shops and a gym in a Gothic Revival church. Back then, the city vibrated. It felt like at any moment something could happen that might change your day or the course of your life. Sometimes, it did.

Manhattan is dangerous, though not for the old reasons: muggings, pickpocketing, prostitution. The danger is that the longer you stay—the longer you're bathed in the glow of blinking screens in Times Square, swept along by swarms of commuters, pursued by a mangy imitation of Mickey Mouse who wants a few dollars to pose for photos—the less you're able to feel the wonder. The lights dim. The little battles with subway doors, your radiator, the rat that walks into you in Union Square as if *you* were the rodent, wear you down. You grow tired, switch off certain receptors.

For years I paid little attention to my city, and in time, it disappeared. I put on sunglasses, put in earbuds, and blindly walked the streets that Billie Holiday and Roy Lichtenstein had walked. Every parade was an inconvenience, as was every stranger, talking too loudly, walking too slowly. I was living in one of the most visited cities in America, working in a skyscraper that people from all over the world stopped to photograph, and skipping town whenever possible.

After my return to Paris, one thing seemed obvious: To see Manhattan again, to feel as good about New York as Liza Minnelli sounded singing about it at Giants Stadium in 1986 (Google it), I had to start treating it as if it were a foreign city; to bring a reporter's eye and habits, care, and attention to daily life.

But as that was the sort of vague self-directive easily ignored, I gave myself a specific assignment: Once a week, during routine errands, I would try something new or go someplace I hadn't been in a long while. It could be as quick as a walk past the supposedly haunted brownstone at 14 West 10th Street, where former resident Mark Twain is said to be among the ghosts. It could be a stroll on the High Line, the elevated park with birch trees and long grasses growing where freight trains used to roll. Or it could be a snowy evening visit to the New York Public Library's Beaux-Arts flagship on Fifth Avenue, where Pamuk wrote the first sentence of *The Museum of Innocence*. There I wandered past white marble walls and candelabras, under chandeliers and ornate ceiling murals, through the room with more than ten thousand maps of my city, eventually taking a seat at a communal wood table to read a translation of Petrarch's *Life of Solitude,* too rare to be lent out.

Tourist Tuesdays I called these outings, to no one but myself. I chose that particular day not for alliterative kicks but because it was the one I had set aside to run routine errands. Decades of research by B.J. Fogg, the director of the persuasive technology lab at Stanford University, suggests that new habits are most effectively formed if you start small and attach them to already existing practices, or "anchors," as he calls them, like brushing your teeth or picking up the mail.

So began my experiments as a hometown tourist. Throughout the winter I made weekly getaways, be it to the food hall in the basement of the Plaza hotel or to the World Trade Center Transportation Hub where, standing on platforms cantilevered over the main hall, I floated between its colossal white steel ribs, like Jonah in the belly of the giant fish. At the Strand bookstore I discovered Jean-Paul Aron's account of eating in nineteenth-century France. At the Jefferson Market Library—the Victorian redbrick Gothic building with a turreted bell and clock tower in Greenwich Village—I paused before vivid stained-glass windows. The building had the trappings of a church, though rare is a house of worship with a Mae West community room upstairs (giving a wholesome spin to her line "Why don't you come up sometime and see me"). Indeed, the library had not been a church, but a courthouse and a prison, where West herself had been jailed for an obscene performance in a play called *Sex*. Who knows how many times I'd walked by those stained-glass windows on the street, never bothering to find out what was on the other side. I had never followed the winding stairs up to the bell tower or down to the graceful brick arches of the basement reference room and the library's Greenwich Village collection, which featured books like *Haunted Greenwich Village* and *Boss Tweed's New York*.

On those Tuesdays I became a student, learning that in the city's museums and libraries you could find van Gogh's *Starry Night;* an autographed manuscript of a Mozart symphony; and, afloat in the Hudson River, a nuclear missile submarine. In the offices of my own newspaper, from which Times Square takes its name, I stopped to admire Hirschfeld drawings and historic maps, and the writing desk of Henry J. Raymond, a founder in 1851 of the *New-York Daily Times.* I looked closer, went slower, read about local lore. Buying physical books, touching paper, made it easier to savor. I spread out a map, reminding myself of the city's shape, its arteries and possibilities. Almost every street has a story. Knowing even a little about them refreshed places that were so familiar I had stopped seeing them.

I began reading about urban planning, a subject that had long interested me. To fall in love with your city again, try seeing it through the eyes of an urbanist. You become a benevolent narrator, observing how your characters negotiate daily routines as they hurry about their lives. You come to understand how a new building affects a nearby park, how a few chairs placed under a tree can transform a street. Even things that are irritating—the biker flying down the sidewalk, the plaza with no place to sit—become a puzzle to solve. What design might be better? What would bring everyone together? What pulls them apart? The spirit of investigation began to return, and I was back on the sidewalk, looking for clues.

Research shows that not long after we get home from a vacation, we tend to return to our particular baseline level of happiness. To help prevent that from happening, I didn't fully leave the cities I'd visited but instead made them filters through which I saw my own. I stopped into small bread and cheese shops, took my time with my coffee. Seemingly cheerless streets became opportunities for observing graffiti and strangers, for "coloring the external world with the warm hues of the imagination," as Anthony Storr described creative living. Avenue by avenue, through old streets and fresh snow, churchyards, coffee shops, and independent bookshops, Manhattan came into view again.

I began to see it when I began treating my hometown just as I had treated any other city I visited; as if there were only so much time to drink it in.

———

It was on one of these Tuesdays that I remembered I lived on an island. If you've ever seen an aerial photo of Manhattan, this likely strikes you as absurd. But a daily life spent in subway tunnels underground and in canyons between buildings that loom like fortresses can easily make you feel landlocked. High-rises are being made ever higher, so though you may be near one of the rivers that surround the borough, you can't see them. And getting to them isn't necessarily easy or pleasant. You may have to cross a highway only to find yourself standing on a sliver of asphalt, or behind a chain-link fence, or being blasted by the wind from the blades of a helicopter as it takes off for someone's country house. So yes, it's possible to forget that Manhattan was once a maritime city, a place with high tides and Atlantic sturgeon; where men were "fixed in ocean reveries," as Melville put it; where the word "skyscraper" originally referred not to something rooted in the ground, but to the topsail of a clipper ship.

And had it not been for a Tourist Tuesday at the Guggenheim, I might still think of my city's essential elements as concrete and steel. Friends had been talking about an Agnes Martin retrospective at the museum, which led me to go online and reserve a ticket. Hours later, as I stepped up to the information desk inside the Frank Lloyd Wright building among the mansions of Fifth Avenue, it struck me that this was the first time I was visiting a museum alone in my own city.

How could that be? I began ticking off in my head my solo museum trips: the Barnes in Philadelphia, the National Gallery of Art in Washington, D.C., the Jewish Historical Museum in Amsterdam, the Museo Nacional del Prado in Madrid . . . but none in New York, home to Museum Mile.

It was opening hour, and a number of visitors, many of them locals like me, were there on their own in half-open coats, silhouetted by Martin's stark grids and stripes.

"I've lived alone all of my life but I didn't get lonely," Martin once said in an interview at her studio in Taos, New Mexico, her home on and off throughout her career. "I thought I was lucky. The best things in life happen to you when you're alone."

I used to live alone in a studio on the Upper West Side of Manhattan, where the sidewalks were reminiscent of suburbia, populated by dogs, double-wide strollers, and children on Razor scooters. The Upper West Side is where once a year the colossal characters for the Macy's Thanksgiving Day parade lie in puddles in the streets until helium courses through them and they rise like giants. It's where dinosaurs decorate the steps of the American Museum of Natural History at Christmastime; where street signs on 84th Street near the site of Edgar Allan Poe's old farmhouse have twice misspelled his middle name as "Allen," leading a magazine editor to quip that "if the ghost of Poe is wondering when posterity will learn to spell his name correctly, the answer would seem to be: nevermore." The Upper West Side is where orbs representing stars and planets float inside the giant glass cube of the Rose Center for Earth and Space. It's where life-size statues of Frederick Douglass and Abraham Lincoln—who stands on the sidewalk in a stovepipe hat like a ghost after dark—greet you outside the New-York Historical Society, the city's oldest museum.

At the top of the Guggenheim rotunda, Martin's later works called to mind children's wallpaper, and flags I saw on boats in Montauk at the end of summer. I liked these bolder paintings best. A museum booklet explained that they were reminiscent of the paintings from Martin's first years in New York on Coenties Slip, the street she lived on, a place I'd never heard of.

That evening, back at home, I looked it up. Coenties Slip is still there, at the southern tip of Manhattan, near the East River, on a landfill that was once a busy berth for wooden ships arriving from far-flung places. The romanticism of this bygone port of call lured me in. And so on another Tuesday, I bundled up and took the 1 train to the tip of Manhattan, where ferries depart for the Statue of Liberty and the streets date to the city's earliest days.

The subway doors opened at the old South Ferry stop, the last on the line, where on the wall a colorful ceramic tile from the early 1900s was decorated with a sailboat. Outside, the air downtown was colder off the water; the wind stronger, lifting gulls flying in arcs around the Staten Island Ferry Terminal sign. The sun was white and faint in the sky. Men called to visitors standing around stubborn mounds of dirty snow. "Excuse me—sir, ma'am—do you need help?" they asked. "Statue of Liberty? This way."

I hurried away from the ferry ticket sellers, passing shredded plastic bags hanging like cobwebs from bare tree branches in the Battery, and made my way toward the squat old buildings nestled in the valleys between skyscrapers. It was here that George Washington bid his troops farewell at the end of the Revolutionary War and, not too far away, that Thomas Edison's electric plant—supplying the first Edison underground central station system in the country—began operating in 1882.

On Pearl Street, near a Le Pain Quotidien and the remnants of an eighteenth-century cistern, I saw a sign: Coenties Slip.

Melville mentions the Slip in *Moby-Dick* but in *Redburn: His First Voyage* describes it more vividly, so much so that standing on the street that winter morning, I could picture it as having been "somewhere near ranges of grim-looking warehouses, with rusty iron doors and shutters, and tiled roofs; and old anchors and chain-cable piled on the walk"; as a place where "sunburnt sea-captains" could be seen "smoking cigars, and talking about Havanna, London, and Calcutta."

There was no sign of them now—no anchors, no talk of far-away places—only a few restaurants and an eyebrow threading salon. Across the street was Coenties Slip park, which is an ambitious name for a tiny plaza with wood benches and a bare tree guarding its perimeter. In the center was a metal and glass sculpture meant to evoke a boat balanced on its end.

There was likewise no trace of Martin or her neighbors, a who's who of American artists: Ellsworth Kelly, James Rosenquist, Charles Hinman, Robert Indiana. They were the first community of New York artists to live in industrial spaces, according to Holland Carter, the former *New York Times* art critic, and rented for a song the empty brick and granite warehouses—few with heat or kitchens—abandoned by the maritime industry as it crept north in the late 1950s. "Each of the artists pursued an individual path," Carter wrote, "treasuring independence, not only from New York School painting but from one another as well."

Indiana rented a top-floor loft on the Slip. From his windows (which he had to install himself) he had a view of the East River, Brooklyn Heights, abandoned piers, and sycamore trees. In the morning he could watch the sun rise through the cables of the Brooklyn Bridge. At night, it didn't matter if there was moonlight—the lighthouse of the nearby seamen's hostel shined through the skylights of his studio.

The lighthouse is now gone, and most of the lofts have been razed. I looked up what it costs to live on the street these days. A one-bedroom walk-up on 2 Coenties Slip last rented for nearly $3,000 a month.

To learn anything about the Slip while you're actually on it requires seeking out a little brown New York Landmarks Preservation sign posted laughably high on a pole. The lettering was so small that to read it, I had to take a photo and enlarge it. The sign didn't mention Martin or Indiana, or any artist, for that matter. It simply noted that the buildings there stand on the earliest New York landfill. What remains of Martin's era is the work of the artists who lived there, like Andy Warhol's film *Eat* (shot at Indiana's studio) and Indiana's *25 Coenties Slip, July 20, 1957*, part of a series of drawings of the area.

The wind was unforgiving. On the other side of a wall—across FDR Drive, beyond a construction site—was the East River. For once, it was close enough. My cheeks were so cold they felt wet, and my fingers had gone numb in my gloves. I began walking away from the river and the Slip, north through the shadowed side streets of the Financial District, along the last vestiges of nineteenth-century New York. I turned left onto Fulton and was soon heading toward the monolith that is One World Trade Center and, in the foreground, the white whale ribs of the World Trade Center Transportation Hub, so big they seemed to reach across the street. To my right was the steeple of St. Paul's Chapel, dwarfed by newer buildings. As I neared the graveyard and the brownstone church, the last colonial-era church left in Manhattan, I couldn't recall ever having set foot inside. I stopped abruptly and crossed Fulton.

It's strange to see a group of headstones tilted amid modern commerce, bookended by a Staples and a Millennium Hilton. In New York our dead are consigned to the boroughs, so we don't see them unless we make a point of visiting. But there, in downtown Manhattan, was an exception—a reminder of the past. And of the inevitable future. Cemeteries in places like Istanbul rest beside mosques and schools, among the living; inescapable *memento mori*.

St. Paul's is a modest churchyard. There are no twisting paths, no tall sculptures creating private sanctuaries. The trees were barren, save for one holding a large bird's nest. The grass was half covered with a layer of snow. The gravestones—thin and round-shouldered, with caps and tympanums—were the color of bark and river stones, some green with algae, some without words.

The first worshippers gathered at St. Paul's in 1766, more than 250 ago, making it one of the city's oldest buildings in continuous public use. I stepped up onto the west porch, passed under the lantern, and went through the double doors. George Washington (in whose boyhood notebooks you'll find the French maxim "'tis better to be alone than in bad Company") prayed here, when there were still orchards and grass rolling down to the river.

The heat indoors felt good after hours of walking in the wind. I tugged off my gloves, flexed my fingers. Unlike city snow, most everything in the church was a fairly pristine white. Glass chandeliers sparkled at the end of long chains. I walked the black-and-white marble tiles along the side aisles where historical photographs and renderings on display charted the chapel's evolution.

After the attacks on the World Trade Center in 2001, St. Paul's served as a relief mission for recovery workers at Ground Zero. Today a small room, the 9/11 Chapel of Remembrance, has glass cases with photos of firefighters, rosaries, and teddy bears—a rainbow one; one dressed as a police officer; one embroidered with "I Heart NY"—that had been given to rescue workers. I touched a pew that still bore traces of the scratches from gear and boots left by relief workers catching a few hours of sleep between shifts.

Outside, I put on my gloves and caught an express train back uptown. There, I made my way toward home, toward the Hudson River, which runs hundreds of miles down from the Adirondack Mountains, along the west side of Manhattan, to the southern tip of the city before disappearing into the Atlantic Ocean.

# Sanctuaries and Strangers

*Designing Home*

*My happiest times were*
*when*
*i was left alone in*
*the house on a*
*Saturday*
> —Charles Bukowski, "My Secret Life"

The first light appears over Central Park. Scarcely a sound comes through the walls or windows—not the neighbor's baby, not a passing car, only the soft, mechanical whir of the city. I hear the belch of the heater as it wakes; feel a draft under the door. There are no lights in the windows in the tower across the way, only the tiny twinkling ones people wind around their balconies. I'm alone with the morning and the first planes gliding in.

They pass a bright dot in the sky that I think is Venus. The word "planet" is derived from an ancient Greek verb that means "to wander," but in winter, I'm content to stay still. And in my study, that's precisely what I do.

I wrap my hands around a cup of matcha tea as snow blows over the water towers on the rooftops. In the study, I'm offstage. I write, nap, book the next trip. I listen to Christine and the Queens; watch the sun rise and become a hot pink smear; light a candle when the sky begins to go dark in the late afternoon.

It was in the study that I watched videos of Julia Child making French onion soup and teaching the finer points of knife sharpening. In the study, I came across the Surrealist Leonora Carrington, and the journals of Edmond de Goncourt, in which he chronicles his meals and theater outings with Flaubert, Oscar Wilde, and Victor Hugo—as well as his first encounters in the studio of "a painter named Degas" and his initial impressions of the Eiffel Tower. ("One could not dream of anything more offensive to the eye of a member of the old civilizations.") In the study, I began keeping a commonplace book with passages, poetry, and quotes from books and papers about things that intrigued me, a practice that dates to the sixteenth century. And speaking of practices, I began jotting down those that, through cities and seasons, helped make my alone time rich and meaningful: snapshotting the moment, trying new things, being present, being playful, communing with art, cultivating anticipation, finding silence, rolling with whatever comes, walking, listening, reminiscing, remembering that everything is fleeting.

Just as primitive man returned to the cave for security and secrecy, as the historian Lewis Mumford wrote, modern man returns to the study, the home office, even indoor privacy spaces with names like the Pause Pod and the Bocchi Tent (the "All-Alone" Tent, as the Tokyo-based news site SoraNews24 translated it). In *House Thinking,* the writer Winifred Gallagher describes primate research from the National Institutes of Health that found that when monkeys were let out of their home cages and into a playground, they periodically decided to return to their nests to check in. Even the outgoing monkeys did so. This had a calming effect: Their levels of cortisol and other measures researchers use to evaluate stress decreased.

"We too are restored by a respite in our safe base," Gallagher said. Rooms matter. Our environments can affect how we think, feel, and behave. For instance, Judith Heerwagen, a psychologist with the United States General Services Administration, has written that a lack of control over our work environment—whether it involves lighting, temperature, ventilation, or privacy—can lead to withdrawal, negative moods, and even physical symptoms like headaches. At home, we often have more control, both physically and psychologically. Gallagher refers to this as psychological customization: creating spaces that help foster whatever mindset or behavior we wish to arouse.

Nathaniel Hawthorne called his study at his home in Concord, Massachusetts, his "sky parlor." Dylan Thomas thought of his writing shack in Laugharne, Wales, as his "water and tree room." Virginia Woolf famously encouraged women to get rooms of their own.

Not all "rooms" are indoors. Thoreau's "withdrawing room" was a pine forest behind his house in the woods in Concord. Indeed, when the United States established a national wilderness preservation system with the Wilderness Act of 1964, it defined "wilderness" not just as wild land, but also land that "has outstanding opportunities for solitude."

All kinds of people need some sort of withdrawing room: introverts, extroverts, introverts who seem like extroverts. Consider Amy Schumer, a self-described introvert who performs live in front of stadium-size crowds. When filming, she retreats to her trailer during lunchtime so she can have time to herself to meditate. During social gatherings, she takes breaks or walks by herself. When she's on the subway, she wears headphones to create a sense of privacy. "I enjoy being alone," she wrote in her book of personal essays, *The Girl with the Lower Back Tattoo*, explaining that she was never happier than when she finally figured that out about herself.

My own study is small. When birds fly by the window, I see their reflection pass over my glass desk as if it were the sky. I wanted it to be a place for both productive work and meditation. And so it's a kind of tabula rasa: white walls, no photos, no art. Yet here and there are traces of where I've been. A bookmark with gold polka dots from the Hôtel Parc Saint Séverin marks a place in the pages of some paperback and will be rediscovered months or years later. Pocket maps with points of interest circled by hotel clerks are tucked into Moleskine notebooks. A *nazar* hangs from a bracket in a closet, along with the white Bensimon sneakers I picked up in Paris. In the narrow breast pocket of my leather jacket is my business card with the address of the Paris hotel I stayed in while on the assignment for the *New York Times* written on the back.

After that trip, I would unzip the jacket pocket every now

and then to tuck a MetroCard inside—and I'd rediscover the card with the Paris address. It was like fishing joy out of my pocket. And so instead of throwing it away, I slid it back in, where it waits to be found again.

———

On a winter afternoon at the Marlton hotel in Greenwich Village, freelancers gather in the lobby around the fireplace, under the coffered ceilings, snug on green velvet couches and upholstered chairs, tapping on laptops, nursing lattes, unhurried by the staff. Let the wind howl. There are few cozier places to be than inside this boutique hotel with patterned rugs and wood-paneled walls, a touch of Paris on 8th Street.

Much of city life, some of it rather private, doesn't take place at home. A room of one's own, after all, is expensive. And so at the Marlton, people settle into club chairs, log on to the free wi-fi, and conduct the day's business, alone together.

It feels liberating to be out in the world as you work, untethered, away from the fluorescent lights of the office and the purr of idle printers. Eventually, someone will come by and ask if you want a menu. "No rush to order," a waiter once said to me. "People always hang out." The sandwiches are hot, the music soft and wistful: "Dark Side of the Moon" by Chris Staples, "Crucify Your Mind" by Rodriguez. The Marlton was once a single-room-occupancy hotel where the likes of Jack Kerouac and Lenny Bruce checked in. Strangers ask to share an outlet or your couch. You exchange a few words about the food, the weather, favorite hotels in other cities. These brief alliances feel good, like the hearth a few feet away.

One of the boons of time on our own is being able to have experiences we don't necessarily have when we're with friends and family—and that includes trying new things and making new connections. Maybe we've decided to travel alone to Provence for a culinary course, or to Sedona for a spa weekend, or to Maui for surf camp—and in the process, we meet other travelers with similar interests and passions. These connections are part of the joy and reward of alone time. By daring to go alone, we have an opportunity to be quiet and reflective, to expand our mind and our experience—and our social network.

Indeed, for those who prefer to spend less time alone, solo travel often leads to just that because it creates opportunities to meet new people and develop friendships. This is but one reason why trying to convince a friend to accompany us on a trip he or she isn't especially interested in, or waiting to meet a significant other before setting off to a place we've longed to go, isn't necessarily a wise approach. Go alone and there's a good chance of finding companions along the way.

Even the most fleeting connections play an important part in solo travel. Generous strangers may be a source of help and support, be it with directions, restaurant recommendations, or friendly conversation. These moments give a solo traveler a welcome dose of company (we are, after all, social beings) in between adventures.

All that being said, we have a tendency to underestimate the pleasure that can come from conversations with strangers. For instance, a field study by Gillian M. Sandstrom of the University of Essex in England, and Elizabeth Dunn at the University of British Columbia, asked customers buying coffee in a busy

Starbucks to either have a genuine social interaction with the barista, as they would with an acquaintance, or to make their interaction as efficient as possible, avoiding unnecessary conversation. Guess who enjoyed their coffee run more? The people who connected with the person who took their order.

A series of nine experiments by Nicholas Epley, a professor of behavioral science at the University of Chicago Booth School of Business, and Juliana Schroeder, an assistant professor at the Haas School of Business at the University of California, Berkeley, found that there's a significant difference between what we think will happen and what actually happens when we talk to strangers. For example, participants in experiments on subways and buses predicted that they would have a more positive commute if they sat alone in solitude than if they had a conversation with a stranger. But, in fact, people had more pleasant commutes when they connected with others, the researchers reported in a paper published in the *Journal of Experimental Psychology: General*.

There's certainly no dearth of happy childhood tales or games that promote the benefits of interacting with others. The independent-minded heroes of adventures far and wide— Pinocchio, Alice, Dorothy Gale, Stuart Little—all relied on help from benevolent strangers. In the board game Tokaido, choosing to meet a stranger along the way always leads to some sort of reward. Alas, in real life, city dwellers nose-to-shoulder in subways and on congested sidewalks are all too adept at acknowledging one another's presence yet not engaging. "We learn to ignore people and to be ignored by them," Alan Westin said, "as a way of achieving privacy."

But as Epley wrote, sometimes our beliefs about what will make us happy are wrong. Strangers give us an opportunity to meet people living entirely different lives from our own. Whether in the hotel lobby, the library, the bar, or on an overnight flight, they can point the way, or add cheer on a winter morning, like the delivery man who called out to me with small-town geniality, "Happy Valentine's Day!" as we passed on the sidewalk. Or the immigrations officer at a New York airport who after handing my passport back greeted me with, "Welcome home," instantly making me feel part of the tribe. New York is where I unpack my bag. It's where I've met most of my favorite people. We, too, were strangers once.

Kio Stark, who taught a course on strangers at New York University's Interactive Telecommunications Program, has said that a "fleeting intimacy" (on the street, on the subway, ride-sharing through UberPool) can make us feel part of a larger community and lead to new perspectives and connections.

Yet for many of us the thought of striking up a conversation with a stranger may be uncomfortable, even anxiety-provoking. And, of course, different cultures have different norms when it comes to such interactions. In the United States, the Project for Public Space has found that when we feel comfortable speaking with strangers, we tend to feel a stronger sense of place or attachment to our communities.

Obviously, technology can help facilitate these connections. Airbnb, for instance, offers its Experiences in the form of local tours and activities, like one in Florence that involves following a member of the Tuscan Truffle Hunters Association through

Sanctuaries and Strangers

the countryside, or one in New York that includes enjoying Latino food and a freestyle rap session in Spanish Harlem. But how do you go about doing so spontaneously?

Stark has some suggestions in her book *When Strangers Meet* and in a related TED Talk. Some exercises are designed to get us accustomed to interacting with others, like smiling when we pass someone, giving someone a compliment about something he or she is wearing, or striking up a conversation not by talking directly to the stranger, but to his or her dog or baby. Another involves what the urbanist William H. Whyte called triangulation: using an object (like a sculpture) or an event (a mime's performance) that both you and a stranger can see, as a jumping-off point for conversation.

It's not uncommon for passing strangers to be privy to confidences that have the feeling of a confessional, one that may not have been shared with friends and family, as the sociologist Georg Simmel described in his early-nineteenth-century essay "The Stranger." After all, the stranger is anonymous. The stranger will move on.

To practice becoming more comfortable with strangers, Stark created a series of urban expeditions that we can try on our own, in order of how challenging they are, at ideas.ted .com/how-to-talk-to-strangers. Some of the cards in the Anywhere Travel Guide card deck (described in the Florence section of this book) may also be helpful: They instruct the reader to stop a stranger and ask what his or her favorite street is, or where to shop or eat. There's an "introduction" card, too, which can be handed to a stranger, allowing for a gracious hello.

219

Opportunities for interactions are all around: in bookshops, with museum security guards, cashiers at grocers, waiters, fellow people in line. Members of a Facebook group called the Community of Single People, created by Bella DePaulo, the researcher and author of *Singled Out,* answered a question I posed about how they meet others by saying it's simply through doing the things they love. A runner said that practically every time he travels alone he participates in a half marathon or marathon: "You've instantly got a common interest."

A woman who likes to bicycle solo said that while she prefers to ride alone "because cycling is, for me, about solitude and meditation, never a social activity," she has no trouble making friends along the way. "Being alone on a bike is all the ice breaker I've ever needed. People are drawn to my adventure and want to be part of it."

While Stark enjoys talking to strangers, she's realistic about the parameters of such experiences. "As a woman, particularly, I know that not every stranger on the street has the best intentions," she said in her TED Talk. "It is good to be friendly, and it's good to learn when not to be, but none of that means we have to be afraid." Although other people may do their best to convince you that you should be fearful: The comedian Jen Kirkman tells a story in one of her stand-up routines about going to Venice by herself. Friends and family expressed a mixture of concern and distaste. "I was excited for this trip before people started putting a damper on it," she says. She then goes on to describe how her father asked why she wasn't afraid to be traveling on her own, raising the specter of ISIS. Her response: "I'm just busy being afraid of plain old men, are you kidding me?"

There's a terrible truth in that. In February 2016, two young female Argentinian backpackers traveling in Ecuador were raped and killed. Much online chatter argued that they shouldn't have been traveling alone. For one thing, they weren't, in fact, alone; they were together. What some critics seemed to be implying is that they shouldn't have been traveling without men. Solo women travelers around the world fired back on social media, posting photos of themselves alone in far-flung places, be it with the Crown Jewels in London or a monkey forest in Ubud, with the hashtag #ViajoSola—"I travel alone."

There's no foolproof set of precautions to take, though experts say that one of our best defenses is something we already have: our gut. Even behavioral science scholars who have studied the benefits of talking to strangers advise against overriding any instincts we have about the safety of a particular situation or another person. "Our intuition often knows what's best for us even when our thinking minds do not understand yet what's going on," as an article in *Psychology Today* put it. (For guidance about safety, see the Tips and Tools section at the back of this book.)

The journalist Stephen J. Dubner, perhaps best known for his collaboration with the economist Steven D. Levitt on *Freakonomics,* has pointed out on his blog that our fear of strangers usually outstrips any actual danger. He's written that in the United States, for instance, crimes such as rape and murder typically involve people the victims know. I'm always cautious, but if I never engaged strangers, I would miss out on a big part of what makes solo travel, not to mention life, fun.

Take, for example, the time I was waiting for my flight to New York from Florence in the Amerigo Vespucci Airport. I noticed a willowy, black-haired woman alone by the gate. When I arrived at my seat, she was in the one beside me. I nodded hello and settled in.

"Are you a journalist or an actress?" she said.

Had I been gifted with the ability to raise an eyebrow, it would have been the perfect occasion.

"Journalist," I said. "How did you know?"

She noticed me as I had noticed her, the way any creature recognizes its own kind. She explained that she had been in Florence writing for a fashion blog and held a stick of gum in my direction. Before long, we were 36,000 feet in the air and talking like friends about our jobs and cities. She was French, living in Paris. We exchanged emails. When we landed at Paris–Charles de Gaulle— me for my connection, she for home—she pointed me toward my connecting flight and hugged me goodbye. *Au revoir.*

She went right; I went left. I pictured us on either side of an ocean, both writing, one awake while the other slept.

A few days after I returned to New York I received an email. Subject: "Let us keep connected." It was from my airplane double. "It's been a real pleasure travelling with you" she wrote. "I would be glad to see you again. Let me know when you are back in Paris."

And just like that—an invitation.

# Ode to the West Village

*I strolled along with my heart expanding at the thought that
I was citizen of great Gotham, a sharer in its magnificence
and pleasures, a partaker in its glory and prestige.*
—O. Henry, "The Four Million"

A city is different things to us at different times—of the day,
of the year, of our life. Many years have passed since I was
in the backseat of the car, taken with the razzle-dazzle. Today,
I'm more drawn to the neighborhood coffee shops, or modest
old parks like Abingdon Square in Greenwich Village, where
farmers come to sell cheese and eggs under the London Plane
trees. I have a soft spot for the little urban islands like McCarthy
Square, with its birdhouses—some with simple peak roofs;
others with multiple stories and decks, made of miniature
wood logs, like ski chalets—that poke out from shrubs and
evergreens. I like the quiet of the West Village in the morning,
where sidewalk chalkboards outside restaurants and coffee

shops promise caffeine and better days, and streets paved with setts—Jane, West 12th, Bethune, Bank—feed into Washington Street like streams emptying into a river.

Downtown, things are of a human scale. The streets are crooked. You aren't oppressed by the city's grid, by vertiginous buildings and long avenues. There are row houses with window boxes and low gates decorated with cobwebs on Halloween and plastic beads on Mardi Gras. You can get pleasantly lost. You can see the sky.

I've lived much of my life on the Upper West Side, but downtown has a particular lure. Because it doesn't conform to Manhattan's grid, it's almost like being in a different city altogether, making the joy of discovery, and all the other virtues of being alone, that much easier to appreciate.

I used to take long walks only in good weather. Now I do so in any weather. When I travel, my favorite way to acquaint myself with a city is to walk it. Why not do the same in my hometown? As of 2017, New York has the highest big-city Walk Score in the nation, a ranking based on a location's population density, block length, distance from amenities, and pedestrian friendliness. I'd always walked a fair amount in Manhattan. But after Paris, Istanbul, and Florence, I ditched my heavy shoulder bag and bought a backpack, which enabled me to walk longer and farther, hands-free, without pain in my shoulder and without worrying that on snowy, slippery nights, I'd lose my balance. On the coldest days I put on fleece and down and took to the streets of Manhattan dressed for the Adirondacks.

Lo and behold, the walking boosted my spirits—if not my style—and possibly my health, too. Commutes by car and mass transit have been shown to increase stress and blood pressure. Off the subway, back on the sidewalk, my cheeks burned from the wind. I got snowed on, rained on, splashed with mud, and arrived everywhere with matted hair and a runny nose and still, I was happier. Research from McGill University published in the journal *Transportation Research* found that of four thousand people who commuted—on foot or by bus, subway, or train—in the midst of a snowy Montreal winter, it was the walkers who had the least stressful commute, despite the weather.

"The heart sees the joy of early dawn, the breeze," wrote Rumi. "What have you seen? What have you not seen?" One reason Village walks are so appealing is how slow the neighborhood can be to wake while the rest of Manhattan is already buzzing, offering an opportunity to savor its little streets, and the time and space for reflection.

Walking through the Village, I took inventory of the changes that had taken place—or not—since my travels. In Paris, Comptoir Turenne was still serving coffee on the sleepy end of the street. In Florence, the seasons were still standing at the corners of the Ponte Santa Trìnita. I still couldn't let go of my iPhone.

Other things were gone. My friends sold the house on the bay. Leonard Cohen died, as had Vito Acconci. Istanbul was rocked by attacks. Today, even as the city is building a state-of-the-art airport, the State Department has warned Americans to reconsider travel to Turkey because of terrorism and travel bans that have prevented them from leaving the country. I have yet to go back.

"One of the laws of travel, one of the laws of the kingdom," Fred Bryant said, "is it must end."

But I still hear the muezzin. I hear the ships' horns, the gull's cry, the ticking of time in the Museum of Innocence. Even in New York, when the snow is falling and crunches softly underfoot, I can summon the sounds of faraway places. I hear Paris: the soft click of a bicycle chain on a sunny afternoon, children playing soccer in the churchyard, spring rain through the open window. I hear the fountains in Florence, footsteps on cobblestones, the nighttime hum of the piazza beyond the shutters.

The experiences we look back on don't have to be extraordinary to be gratifying. In fact, studies by scholars at Harvard Business School published in the journal *Psychological Science* found that we tend to underestimate the pleasure of rediscovering our ordinary, everyday experiences through things like journal entries and letters. We're more apt, however, to chronicle major life events and yearly vacations, not necessarily the quotidian. And that may be a missed opportunity. For instance, in one study the researchers found that university students who had created time capsules of mundane information—notes about recent conversations, social outings, songs they were listening to—had significantly underestimated their interest when they revisited the capsules a mere three months later. Another study found that people underestimated how much pleasure they would get from reading something they wrote about a "typical" experience with their partner.

"We generally do not think about today's ordinary moments as experiences that are worthy of being rediscovered in the future," lead researcher Ting Zhang told the Association for Psychological Science. "However, our studies show that we are often wrong: What is ordinary now actually becomes more extraordinary in the future—and more extraordinary than we might expect."

We can't always escape to Paris or Istanbul. Nor do we always want to. Savoring the moment, examining things closely, reminiscing—these practices are not strictly for use on the road. They're for everyday life, anywhere. In fact, you can begin right now if you like with a savoring practice that Bryant and Veroff created called the Daily Vacation. Here's how it works:

Each day for a week, plan and take a daily vacation by doing something that you enjoy for twenty minutes or more. The vacation can be something as simple as going for a walk around your neighborhood, or thumbing through a book on gardening. Aim to be in the moment, and "to see things as if for the first or last time."

The Daily Vacation can be taken on a shoestring budget, Bryant points out, and there are no security lines to contend with. For him, a Daily Vacation sometimes means making a journey to the past by reminiscing about a former trip. He may "re-enter" that experience by holding a precious, almost sacred, memento, like the diary his father kept when they vacationed together on a mountain in Colorado—just as I may summon Paris by listening to Henri Salvador's "Ma chansonnette," which I once heard at the Relais Christine, a Left Bank hotel housed in a former mansion with cats that flash here and there. To

heighten the effects of the Daily Vacation, Bryant suggests planning the next day's vacation at the end of the current one so
there's something positive to look forward to, as well as something to look back on.

On a winter morning in the Village I went through an iron
gate on Hudson Street into the gardens of the Church of Saint
Luke in the Fields. Snow was thawing on the flowerbeds. "Please
respect the sanctuary of this space," said a sign covered in bare
vines. Visitors were asked not to use cell phones. I stopped beside a bench with a little memorial plaque and bent down to
read the last line of Shelley's "Ode to the West Wind"—"If Winter
comes, can Spring be far behind?"—which he wrote in a wood
that skirts the Arno, near Florence.

With only a few minutes before my first meeting of the day,
I left the garden and walked toward 10th Street, noticing an
empty beer can roll under a parked truck and listening to the
chiming of bells. I passed the red doors to the Three Lives &
Company bookstore on my way to Jack's Stir Brew Coffee.

The wood tables at Jack's are almost always taken when I go,
which is reassuring, as it means the place will likely still be
there when I show up again. I ordered my usual: the Dirty
Harry with almond milk, which is basically a vanilla latte. It's
warm, never hot, instantly ready to meet your lips.

I returned to the sidewalk, cup in hand. The city, my city,
first came into view through a backseat window. It came on
the other side of a long, dim tunnel, in passing flashes of head-
lights, in darkened theaters and restaurants. Now I see it on
foot in the first light, the time of delivery trucks and dog walkers; when a construction site shudders to life with the slow

swing of a crane, everywhere the skeleton of a building getting its skin.

After taking my city for granted, complaining about its pace, its smells, its noise, its people, its anonymous buildings blocking the sky, it's romancing me. I pass the dog walkers, the bridges, the kayakers and houseboats on the Hudson, the *wabi-sabi* streets and stoops, and am thankful that in less than twenty-three square miles the city provides both profound solitude—and also the very best people with whom to break it.

William Whyte, the urbanist who spent more than sixteen years walking and studying the streets of New York, once said that though we may say we wish to get away from it all, in the end we gravitate to the lively spaces, the places where we can see one another. We go there willingly, "not to escape the city," he said, "but to partake of it."

I stuffed a hand into my pocket. The day was chilly, yet there seemed to be the faintest hint of warmth in the air, the promise of a new season. Some people are born knowing how to savor. Others learn. And they can pass it along, Bryant said, from generation to generation.

On West 4th Street sunlight spilled down the ivy on the trunk of an old, tilted tree. Sidewalk tables were being set with folded napkins, as sure a sign of spring as the appearance of crocuses and pine warblers. Men were pouring dirt into planters on the townhouse stoops. Birds made a happy racket in the bushes. And nearby, the tulips poked up in Abingdon Square.

Each day I perform complex choreography around people, dogs, garbage bags, cyclists going the wrong way, traffic signs with arrows that say ONLY, creaking as they swing in the wind.

Sometimes I walk for blocks, even miles, without paying much attention. But then my gait slows. Something tugs at my arm and whispers, *Look! Look. There are limestone angles above the doors of the Parish of the Guardian Angel. There's a Banksy painted on Zabar's. There are toy cardinals tied like red ribbons to tree branches on Bank Street.*

And just like that, Manhattan has me again.

# Tips and Tools for Going It Alone

The following is to help give you a sense of the world of resources out there. It's hardly a comprehensive guide but rather, a departure point: ideas about meeting people on the road, tracking where you're wandering, learning a language, booking a table, chilling out, staying safe, and, of course, giving back. Below are a number of apps and websites, as well as some general travel information. But apps, start-ups, even hotels, come and go, and country laws are evolving, so it's possible that something here has changed by the time you read it. That said, when one app or start-up vanishes, another potentially helpful tool tends to appear in its place. For the most up-to-date information, join me at StephanieRosenbloom.com.

## Stay

There's no standard solo trip or lodging style: Some people want tree houses; others want luxury suites. There's a good deal of information online for solo travelers looking for home swaps (*HomeExchange* is one of the world's largest exchange sites) or budget places to stay (*Couchsurfing* is an established player; *Tentrr* offers campsites bookable online, while *Hipcamp* has sites with lodgings like tents and yurts), and of course there's *Airbnb*. Pod hotels have reasonable rates, too, as do many *ryokans*, which offer both privacy and community.

For those looking for higher-end hotels, in Europe many have lodgings for solo travelers, including the places I stayed. Often called single rooms, they're typically smaller than standard ones but are a way to check in to some of the nicest places for less. One thing to keep in mind: Hotels don't always list their single rooms under the Rooms and Suites section of their websites. You may have to search on a particular date to see prices and availability.

Even if you choose not to stay in a "single" room, hotels that offer and advertise them—such as the Hôtel Parc Saint Séverin, which said on its website that its single rooms are "ideal for your solo stays in Paris," or the Savoy, which described having rooms that are "perfect for the solo traveller"—send an important message: Solo travelers are welcome.

## Play

*Anywhere Travel Guide*. You probably don't want to carry a deck of cards with you when you're walking around, but you can sift through these before you head out the door. The suggestions they offer—"Observe silence today . . . Notice how this changes your impression of the sounds that surround you" or "Eat something you haven't tried before"—are a great way to start thinking differently about how you see, experience, and savor a place, even your own backyard.

*Tokaido*. This board game, by the Paris-based company Funforge (funforge.fr), puts you in the right state of mind for travel by making you think about what you see, eat, give, and encounter along the way. An app allows you to play solo, with up to four artificially intelligent travelers. It's just the thing for long layovers.

*Duolingo.* This free website and app (duolingo.com) turns language learning into a game of multiple-choice questions, word-matching quizzes, and writing and speaking translation challenges. If you answer correctly, you proceed to the next level. It's language learning you can do at home or on the fly—waiting in line at the grocery store, on an airplane, or during your lunch hour. The more you learn, the more virtual currency you receive, which you can use to unlock bonus lessons, like how to flirt in French. The quizzes are short and mildly addictive, which is just what you want when practicing a language. Courses are available in Spanish, German, Japanese, Hebrew, French, Turkish, Italian, and more. A better use of your time than Candy Crush Saga? *Evet,* as they say in Turkish.

*BookCrossing.com.* A terrific solitary activity: "Hide" a book in a park or a city street for someone to find and enjoy. Join Book-Crossing (it's free), which allows you to print a label, attach it to your book, register it, and track where it goes. "Think of it as a passport enabling your book to travel the world without getting lost," the site says. Leave books around your hometown, or like bread crumbs in places you travel. Who knows, maybe you'll find one someday—maybe one that I left for you. (If you're drawn to the chance and sweetness of BookCrossing, you may also like Boom Boom! Cards, each of which instructs you to perform an act of kindness before passing the card on to someone else. Or consider *MoreLoveLetters.com,* which began with one woman leaving letters of encouragement to strangers around New York City. The website allows people to request letters, and volunteer to send notes to those who could use a little cheer.)

## Walk

*LiveTrekker,* created in France, is a free app for *flâneurs* with type-A personalities. Go ahead and stroll wherever the day takes you, and LiveTrekker (livetrekker.com) will follow along in the background, logging how far you walk and drawing a red line up and down the streets and through the gardens and museums you visit, creating a detailed, zoomable map (a satellite view allows you to see landmarks like the Eiffel Tower). You don't need to do a thing or be connected to wi-fi. Just hit start before you go, and the app takes care of the rest. At the end of the day you can see a beautiful map of exactly where you've been. You can even share it with all the people who wish you had invited them along.

*Detour.* This audio tour company (detour.com) offers affordable walking tours of cities including London, Paris, Rome, New York, New Orleans, Portland, and Savannah. In Paris, for instance, you can take a tour of Saint-Germain called "The Golden Age of African-American Writers" that follows the trail of Richard Wright and James Baldwin. Not into audio tours but still want some direction? You may want to look into self-guided walking tours from companies like *Country Walkers,* which include maps, itineraries, luggage transfers, breakfasts, and some other meals.

*Google Maps.* When you're someplace unfamiliar and want to find a good place to eat, touch this app's "Explore" icon, where you can choose from categories like "lunch," "coffee," "dinner," "cheap eats," and "vegetarian-friendly spots." The map's navigation and turn-by directions are on point, but there are also detailed off-line maps of many cities so you don't have to run up your data bill each time you need directions.

Traveling abroad? You may also want to add the *Google Translate* app to your phone. It's allowed me to converse with Japanese taxi drivers, read French museum signs, and order dinner in Italian. It can be used in a variety of ways. The method I turn to most often involves the camera icon. Just tap it and hold your phone over a menu to see a virtual-reality translation, or take a snapshot of whatever text you're looking at and the app will translate it. You can get translations of words that you speak, type, or draw on your smartphone screen with your finger. The app is also capable of translation while two people converse. All that, and it's free.

## Meet

In addition to striking up conversations on the fly, there are all sorts of ways to meet locals and fellow solo travelers. Some cities have free greeter programs, like Brisbane Greeters in Australia. The *Global Greeter Network* (globalgreeternetwork.info) includes cities like New York, Chicago, Tokyo, Buenos Aires, Naples, and Haifa.

Looking to tour with other solo travelers? *Context Travel* (contexttravel.com) offers private or group walking tours (for no more than seven people) in more than thirty cities around the world, led by scholars with advanced degrees. *Overseas Adventure Travel* (oattravel.com) caters to travelers over fifty with small-group itineraries and has seen the number of solo travelers mushroom in recent years—it expects that soon about half of its travelers will be solos. In 2016, *Intrepid Travel* (intrepidtravel .com), with headquarters in Australia, began offering solo-only tours. Their popularity led the company to offer half a dozen solo-only departures to places like Bali and Morocco in 2018. *Road Scholar* (roadscholar.org) specializes in educational trips and offers solo travelers their own rooms for no supplemental charge.

If you don't want to travel with others throughout your entire vacation, you may prefer day tours and experiences, which are increasingly popular among solo travelers. Websites that offer activities with locals or guides come and go. *Toursbylocals .com* has been around since 2008. *MeetUp.com,* which has been sold to WeWork (see p. 246), has been organizing group activities for more than a decade and is a nice way to meet others who share your interests, be that going for a hike or visiting museums. Airbnb began offering what it calls Experiences (airbnb.com/experiences)—day tours and workshops led by locals in cities throughout the world (Havana, New Delhi, Tokyo, London), many for prices that won't bust your wallet, and are available to anyone, not just travelers renting its homes. *TripAdvisor* has also gotten into the game, offering tours and activities bookable at tripadvisor.com/attractions (the company's website has a solo travel forum, too).

Also check out robust solo travel communities like *Solo Travel Society* on Facebook and the related website, *Solo Traveler*, at solotravelerworld.com.

## Eat

If you want to break up a solo vacation by sharing a meal (and perhaps learn a thing or two about local cuisine), you may want to consider wine appreciation classes and tastings, cooking classes—in Paris you can take them at schools from chefs like *Alain Ducasse* (ecolecuisine-alainducasse.com)—and gastronomic walking tours with stops at markets, bakeries, and pâtissieries. For instance, *Paris by Mouth* (parisbymouth.com) offers small-group food and wine tours like "Taste of the Marais" and "Taste of Saint-Germain." If you prefer to explore markets on your own, the *Marchés de Paris* app (marchesdeparis.com/en) allows you to search the city for food, flower, flea, and bird markets. You can narrow your results by day of the week and market type (including whether it's indoors or outdoors and has organic food) and see which fruits and vegetables are in season. Cost: $0.99.

Another way to find market tours and classes, or just someone with whom to share a meal, is through peer-to-peer apps and websites, which enable you to book meals with local hosts in a matter of minutes. Some hosts are even professional chefs. *Feastly* (eatfeastly.com), for instance, is entirely made up of them. *EatWith* (eatwith.com) offers meals in more than two hundred cities, including San Francisco, New York, Tel Aviv, Rome, and Barcelona. *Withlocals* (withlocals.com) focuses on food and cultural experiences in places like Asia (including Cambodia, Indonesia, and Vietnam), the Netherlands, Spain, Greece, England, Belgium, and Portugal. Other examples include *Meal Sharing, VoulezVouzDîner,* and *BonAppetour.* You may want to visit the social media pages and blogs of these companies of these companies as well, because they can be a source of inspiration and information about ways to meet people. Also, *TripAdvisor* features bookable "food tours" listings on its site.

As with other peer-sharing sites like Airbnb, you rely on user reviews and the host's profile page to inform your selection. Some hosts cook for two or three people; others for half a dozen. So you may not be dining only with the chef, but perhaps his or her spouse, as well as other travelers or even locals in the mood for a home-cooked meal. Prices vary greatly, not just from city to city but within cities. You can find meals for $35 or for $135, depending on factors including the food being served, the location, and the chef's experience.

As homey and genial as these sites look, remember that while some verify basic information (like names, social media profiles, addresses, and payment information), they generally do not run comprehensive background checks on the people whose homes you're visiting. So read the reviews and any biographical information the hosts provide carefully. (Some may offer links to their culinary work or social networks.) You may also be able to message the chef or host before booking a meal to ask for more information and get a feel for him or her. Some sites, like Feastly, don't just have shared meals at the cook's home but also offer them at pop-up locations, farms, and other large venues.

Prefer a table for one? A booking app like *TheFork* (thefork .com, owned by TripAdvisor), can help make such a reservation in places throughout Europe (France, Italy, Spain, Portugal, Netherlands) when you don't speak the language and aren't staying at a hotel where someone can book a table for you. You can also browse menus, photos, and reviews. Does TheFork have all the hottest restaurants? No. But as with popular U.S. booking apps like *Resy* or *OpenTable* (which has very few restaurants in places like Paris, Florence, and Istanbul), it has some good spots and it's a breeze to use.

## Chill

If you're looking to meditate, practice being in the moment, or simply unwind when you're on your own, these apps and websites are one way your smartphone may actually help.

*Insight Timer.* There are many fine meditation apps, but this one (insighttimer.com) is free, has thousands of guided meditations, and is customizable. You can set a timer for how long you want to meditate, add some bells at chosen intervals, ambient sound and music—or silence—and meditate on your own.

*Calm.* This app and website (calm.com) offer various guided meditations, but you may like Calm just for the free nature sounds and videos—beach waves, rain on leaves, a crackling fire—that beat the drone of white noise any day. When you're on the road alone or working and need to drown out the masses, this is a good one to have in your arsenal.

*Breathe 11:11.* At 11:11 a.m. in your local time zone, this free app will chime and you'll receive a notification on your phone that says "Breathe. Wish. Connect." (Presumably along with others who have downloaded the app—you can see a heatmap of where in the world people are using it.) The idea is to encourage mindful breathing and positive thinking, to use the moment to take at least three slow, deep breaths. (If 11:11 a.m. isn't convenient, you can set the chimes to go off at a different time. You can also change the notification to something more personal if you prefer.)

*Productive.* This app allows you to set reminders throughout the day, week, or month to do things like take a breath, write in your journal, get outside, even "talk to a stranger." Suddenly a little bell and banner on your phone will remind you to breathe, stretch, or engage in whatever habits you've added from the app. You can also write in your own. In this way, even if you have only a minute to yourself, you can use it meaningfully. Users can schedule a few habits free of charge, but if you want to add others, and receive timed reminders and weekly stats about how you're doing, you'll have to upgrade to a subscription (about $4 a month; $10 for six months; $20 for a year). Productive is hardly the only game in town, so be sure to check out the competition, including apps like *HabitMinder* and *Habitica* (which turns establishing habits into a game by giving you rewards like virtual pets), before deciding.

*Headspace.* Andy Puddicombe's soothing English accent and affable demeanor are likely to make even the most reticent meditators give the practice a second try. Headspace (head space.com) includes short sessions that make it easy to fit meditation into your schedule. There's a ten-day free trial; after that, you pay by subscription type (about $13 a month; $72 a year; or $400 a lifetime).

*Freedom.* Hoping to get into a flow state? This program (free dom.to) will block websites and apps on your smartphones, tablets, and computers so you can stay focused (about $7 a month; $29 a year; $129 forever).

*Coffitivity.* Like Calm, this app and desktop tool (siwalik.in /coffitivityoffline) provides ambient noise—in this case, the sounds of a coffee shop—that its makers say will help boost your creativity. Whether or not that proves to be true, it's another pleasing alternative to white noise. You can choose from free soundtracks like "morning murmur" and "university undertones," or buy additional "premium" coffee shop ambiences such as "Brazil Bistro" and "Texas Teahouse."

*Pause.* The makers of this seemingly simple app say it uses principles of Tai Chi to help you relax and focus your attention. Think of it as guided meditation through images instead of voice. Just place your finger on a small blob and slowly move it around the screen of your smartphone. Move gently, and the blob grows while your ears are bathed with ambient sound, birdsong, and the sound of breaking waves. Move too quickly and the app (ustwo.com/work/pause-app) tells you to slow down. I was skeptical, but it's one of the few digital tools that in as little as a minute successfully forces me to, well, pause (about $2).

*ASMR videos.* ASMR stands for something that sounds scientific—Autonomous Sensory Meridian Response. For the uninitiated, it's a feeling of relaxation, often described as tingles, that some people get when they hear soft sounds like whispers and gentle tapping, or see slow or repetitive movements like fluttering hands. Sometimes these videos take the form of role plays in which the viewer receives a virtual shoulder massage or is welcomed to a luxury hotel. There are people all over the world who make free YouTube videos of these prompts designed to help others relax. Many people simply use the videos as sleep aids. Just Google ASMR, choose the "videos" category, and you'll be on your way. You can also watch and listen in other languages, like French (try the Made in France ASMR and Paris ASMR YouTube channels).

## Be Safe

A few preventative measures and some common sense can go a long way toward reducing any risks while traveling.

*Learning the Laws and Customs of Your Destination.* The U.S. State Department offers information about cultural norms, laws, crime, health considerations, visa requirements, embassy locations, and the use of drugs and alcohol for countries around the world at travel.state.gov. The site also has additional tips for specific types of travelers, including women, people with disabilities, and LGBTI travelers.

Lesbian, gay, bisexual, and transgender tourism has experienced a significant increase in recent years, according to a 2017 report by the World Tourism Organization and the International Gay & Lesbian Travel Association. Yet the report notes that there are still dozens of countries where homosexuality is criminalized and, in some places, punishable by death. Several websites offer detailed information, including the International Lesbian, Gay, Bisexual, Trans and Intersex Association (ILGA), which has maps that chart where criminalization, protection, and recognition laws exist. You can learn more at ilga.org

/maps-sexual-orientation-laws. *ManAboutWorld,* a digital travel magazine written by gay men, has an LGBTQ safety guide at manaboutworld.com/lgbtq-travel-safety. The editors there have also pointed out that dating apps may be useful. *SCRUFF,* for instance, has *SCRUFF Venture* (support.scruff.com), which allows users to get advice and recommendations from locals and fellow travelers before and during a trip.

*Signing Up for Safety Alerts.* If you're a United States citizen, one of the easiest things you can do is register your trip (for free) with the Smart Traveler Enrollment Program, known as STEP. Doing so enables citizens and nationals to receive emails from the nearest embassy about safety conditions in your destination country so you can make up-to-the-minute decisions about your travel plans. It also enables the embassy or consulate as well as friends and family to contact you in an emergency, be it a natural disaster or civil unrest. (This is how I received timely security alert emails about Istanbul.) You can sign up at step.state.gov/step. Additionally, look up the phone number and address of the nearest embassy in the country you're visiting and write it down in advance of your trip in case of an emergency.

Social networking sites can also be essential tools. Following the right accounts on *Twitter* can provide the most up-to-the-minute information, be it about hurricanes (the National Oceanic and Atmospheric Administration's National Weather Service account is @NWS) or health (the Centers for Disease Control & Prevention main account is @CDCgov). When traveling, follow government agencies and the tourism board to stay in the loop (you can always unfollow them when you return home). Even if you're not a member of Airbnb, it may be helpful to follow @AirbnbHelp: During emergencies and disasters, like the earthquake in Mexico in September 2017, Airbnb has helped people find temporary accommodations as part of its disaster response program.

In an emergency like an earthquake or mass shooting, *Facebook* activates its Safety Check tool (facebook.com/about/crisis response), which allows users to let their friends and family know they're safe and to see if others are safe as well.

*Getting Health Coverage.* Your regular health insurance may cover some of your care if you're abroad, but call your provider before your trip to find out. When I did so, I got such vague answers that I realized it was best for me to get supplemental insurance. Especially important for adventure travelers, people with preexisting conditions, and those journeying to remote places is evacuation insurance. Few health insurance companies will pay for medical evacuation back to the United States, which can cost $50,000 or more, according to the State Department. A recent search for an annual membership in an air medical transport program (with at least $100,000 in evacuation coverage) that would include repatriation to the hospital of my choice in the United States for my trips throughout the year was about $100 to $270. (Some of the policies also included nonmedical evacuation to a place of safety in the event of political or civil unrest during the trip.)

Travel insurance comparison sites like *Squaremouth* and *InsureMyTrip* enable you to filter and compare different insurance policies across multiple providers to find the best plan for your particular needs. Squaremouth recommends having a policy with at least $50,000 in emergency medical coverage (reimbursement for the cost of treatment while traveling) for international travel, and at least $100,000 for cruises or travel to remote locations. A "primary" policy, the company said, allows you to bypass your health insurance and claim directly through your travel insurance policy. (A "secondary" policy can be less costly, though it adds another potentially time-consuming step to the claims process.) In 2017, Squaremouth said the least expensive "primary" policy on its website for two fifty-year-olds taking a ten-day domestic road trip was $42—a small price to pay to make sure you get the care you need.

*Minding What You Put Online.* If you're posting travel photos and updates to social media, make sure you're not sharing information that could put you at risk. If you check in somewhere or have location services enabled on your mobile phone photos, you're broadcasting your location, possibly making you or your home a target.

*Staying in Touch.* While you should limit what you post publicly, keeping close friends and family in the loop about where you are and when you'll check in is a smart idea. Just be thoughtful about with whom you share your information. To that end, you can keep in touch through a communications app like *WhatsApp,* which allows users to avoid SMS fees by using only the phone's Internet connection to send messages or make voice and video calls.

*Doing Your Research.* One of the joys of traveling is figuring things out as you go. But when it comes to logistics, some light homework—about dress codes and transportation, for example—can keep headaches and trouble at bay. For instance, familiarizing yourself with the transportation options available at a particular airport can make for a smoother arrival and help ensure that you won't get into a car with someone who might try to charge more than you ought to be paying. You may also want to write down the address of your destination in case you need directions, particularly if you're going to a country where you don't speak the language. You may think your pronunciation is spot-on, but sometimes looking at an address is easier for the person trying to help you.

## Work

For those times when you need more than what a coffee shop can provide (like mail service, a shredder, or an ergonomically friendly chair), there are coworking spaces like *Coworkshop* in Paris, where you can work alone yet also socialize or collaborate with a community of entrepreneurs and freelancers.

*WeWork* (wework.com) has communal workspaces in Paris and cities around the world, including in places like the United States, Canada, the United Kingdom, Germany, Israel, and China. WeWork's least expensive membership is the "hot desk" package, which guarantees a workspace in a common area at one location. (Designated desks and private office packages are more expensive.) The cost includes amenities like office supplies, access to a microwave and a refrigerator, and refreshments like coffee and tea.

To see if coworking spaces are in your area just Google "coworking" and the name of your city. You can do the same if you're interested in exploring cohousing or coliving spaces, some of which do double duty as informal incubators. But lately, a new breed of company has emerged, designed to provide digital nomads—people who chose to travel full time and work remotely—with resources to live and work (wi-fi, local SIM cards) far from home. *Unsettled* (beunsettled.co), for instance, is one such business. It organizes affordable, month-long coworking retreats with shared workspaces and events (dinner parties and weekend explorations), but private accommodations in places such as Colombia, Peru, Morocco, Argentina, Spain, Bali, Portugal, and South Africa.

## Give

Having time to yourself can be wonderful. But for some people, solitude is not a choice. Another way to spend your alone time? Help someone else.

There are countless ways to be of service, including spending time with people who could use a little company. For instance, in the United Kingdom (where in 2018 Prime Minister Theresa May appointed a minister for loneliness to help combat the issue), the charity *Contact the Elderly* (contact-the-elderly .org.uk) organizes free monthly tea parties for people seventy-five and older who live alone. You can volunteer to drive attendees to and from an event, or host one yourself. And the charity *Age UK* (ageuk.org.uk) offers "befriending services" that pair volunteers with older people who would like companionship.

One way to find opportunities to help in your hometown is to search websites like idealist.org. When I typed the word "company" under "volunteer opportunities," for example, one of the first items that turned up was a group that matches isolated seniors with volunteers who make weekly visits. You can also usually find volunteer opportunities by checking your city government website.

Another way to give is to get involved with the placemaking movement, which encourages people to make their local public spaces inviting and meaningful by organizing activities such as block parties or "porchfests," setting up free book exchange stations, helping create public art, and improving community squares. You can learn more at pps.org.

Of course, there are also an infinite number of simple, spur-of-the-moment things you can do when you're on your own, limited only by your creativity: Pay the admission fee for the people behind you, share your umbrella, hold the door, give flowers, offer a compliment, or help someone out so that he or she, too, can enjoy a little alone time.

# Acknowledgments

Thank you to Jay Mandel, my agent at William Morris Endeavor, for believing in me and in this project, for his indispensable guidance, patience, and ideas.

To Rick Kot and the dream team at Viking: I still can't believe my good fortune. Rick is the kind of editor a writer is lucky to have the chance to work with once in a career. To benefit from his poetic touch, astute observations, and elegant solutions on a first book has been an unimaginable gift. I am deeply grateful for his sensibilities, intelligence, humor, and generosity of spirit.

Thank you to Viking president and publisher Brian Tart, to Andrea Schulz, editor in chief, and Lindsay Prevette, director of publicity, as well as the designers, copy editors, marketing team, and especially to Nayon Cho, Christina Caruccio, and my publicist and fellow solo traveler, Brianna Linden. Special thanks to Diego Nunez for being such a class act.

Thank you to the team at WME, including Janine Kamouh, and to Matilda Forbes Watson for deftly shepherding the book across the pond. Lauren Shonkoff is an absolute pro who made a newbie feel at ease. To the wonderful team at Transworld

Publishers, Penguin Random House UK, especially my thoughtful editor, Andrea Henry, and my publicist, Hayley Barnes, whose creativity, hard work, and enthusiasm were palpable even though they were thousands of miles away.

At the *New York Times*, Monica Drake, head of the Travel section, is as smart and perceptive a manager as one could hope for. That this book got finished is thanks to her generosity, for not only giving me the time to go and write it, but for being in my corner.

Suzanne MacNeille gave me Paris—though even Paris pales in comparison to what she gives me every day as my editor in Travel: encouragement, bright ideas, books, and a friendship that has spanned seasons. Stories, not only mine, are made better by her finely tuned ear and knowledge of places near and far. This book exists in no small part because of her.

Thank you to Neil Amdur, who eighteen years ago opened the door for me to the *Times*, and to Dean Baquet, Jill Abramson, and Arthur Sulzberger, Jr. and A.G. Sulzberger who kept it open. I'm deeply grateful to all the editors I've had there.

Trish Hall was among the first, and ever since has been a mentor, model, creative force, and wise voice at the other end of the line, for me and for countless journalists. A special thank-you to her and to Larry Wolhandler for their warmth, friendship, and house by the bay.

I'm thankful to Jerry Gray, Joseph Berger, Bill Brink, Mark Prendergast, Jeff Rubin, Trip Gabriel, Glenn Kramon, Bill Goss, Stuart Emmrich, Erika Sommer, and George Gustines for giving me early opportunities. Thanks to Danielle Mattoon, Rick Berke, and Adam Bryant for my boarding pass to the Travel section, and to my colleagues there—Steve Reddicliffe, Dan Saltzstein, Lynda Richardson, John Dorman, Phaedra Brown, and Rodrigo Honeywell—who make the work fun (as did Seth Kugel). Thank you to the editors on the features copy desk from whom I've learned so much. Thanks to Phil Corbett and Ron Lieber for book-life advice; and to Tony Cenicola, for making me look good.

I am indebted to the scholars whose work enriches these pages.

Fred Bryant's groundbreaking research about savoring is surpassed only by his beautiful storytelling about its practice. Talking with him was one of the most pleasurable and mean-ingful parts of reporting this book.

Bella DePaulo, whose research, books, and articles about single life have long been ahead of their time, was an essential and inspiring source. She could not have been more generous with studies, links, and leads.

Elizabeth Dunn is a leading happiness researcher, author, professor, and adventurer—and yet somehow still made time to answer all my questions about her latest, fascinating work.

Thank you to John Haskins, who taught me how to fly solo, yet has always made sure that the most fun is had when we're together. And to my dear friend Rusty O'Kelley, for his insights and generosity (including sharing John).

*Merci* to David and Susan Liederman who, ever since we met in a restaurant in the 7th arrondissement, have been sharing their delightful stories and expertise about food, wine, and France, but most important—their friendship.

Tim Ferriss provided early, invaluable counsel about book-writing (and just about everything else). Pauline Frommer has long been an inspiration, and I am grateful for her time and thoughtfulness. Carol Gillott showed me around her Paris, imparting her knowledge of cheese and éclairs. Don Frantz showed me the joys of getting lost. Vivian Toy kept me sane and supplied with chocolate. Rachel Brodie sat with me, sometimes on the East Coast, sometimes on the West, sparking essential conversations, and following up with postcards and packages of inspiration.

Many thanks to the friends who contributed advice, gave recommendations, or lent an ear, especially Guy Trebay, Charlie Herman, John Dietrich, Chris Widney, Catherine Saint Louis, Natasha Singer, Simone Oliver, Lisa Perriera, Jacob Bernstein, Jad Mouawad, Alexandra Jacobs, Steve Berman, Michele Sacharow, Shannon Bell, Chris White, Jonathan Fuchs, Larry Rand, Nathan Englander, Rachel Silver, MaMerle and the Thanksgiving crew, Peter, and the Ramah gang. Thanks to Allen Salkin and Kiri Tannenbaum for providing encouragement, cheer, and a room at the beach during formative years.

My family—East Coast Adam, West Coast Adam, Keren, Ella, Sophia, Ariella, Doug, Jessica, Ben, Catherine, Joe, Erica, and the Rosenblooms—gives so much love I never feel alone, even when I am.

Speaking of love:

To my father, who taught me about architecture.

To my mother, who taught me about books.

And to my husband, Daniel—who taught me how to savor.

# Notes

Introduction: Witches and Shamans

1 **"waking time alone":** Mihaly Csikszentmihalyi, *Flow: The Psychology of Optimal Experience* (New York: HarperCollins e-books, 1990).

2 **today to 2030:** "Households in 2030: Rise of the Singletons," *Euromonitor International*, March 20, 2017.

2 **travelers than ever:** Airbnb, "Flying Solo: Trending Destinations & Experiences for Solo Travelers," June 22, 2017, https://press.atairbnb .com/flying-solo-trending-destinations-experiences-solo-travelers/.

2 **first solos only tours:** Company email exchange with the author, December 11, 2017.

2 **organizations, MMGY Global:** MMGY Global Portrait of American Travelers, 2016–17, https://www.mmgyglobal.com/services/research/portrait-of-american-travelers.

3 **completely alone sometimes:** Mary Madden and Lee Rainie, "Americans' Views About Data Collection and Security," Pew Research Center, May 20, 2015, http://www.pewinternet.org/2015/05 /20/americans-views-about-data-collection-and-security/.

3 **also by themselves:** Euromonitor International Global Consumer Trends survey, 2015, https://blog.euromonitor.com/2016/02/top -6-insights-from-the-2015-global-consumer-trends-survey.html.

3 **to accompany them:** Rebecca K. Ratner and Rebecca W. Hamilton, "Inhibited from Bowling Alone," *Journal of Consumer Research* 42, no. 2 (August 2015): 266–83.

3 **"Only witches and shamans":** Csikszentmihalyi, *Flow*.

4   **for fifteen minutes:** Timothy D. Wilson, David A. Reinhard, Erin C. Westgate et al., "Just Think: The Challenges of the Disengaged Mind," *Science* 345, no. 6192 (July 2014): 75–77.

4   **happy, healthy lives:** Robert Waldinger, "What Makes a Good Life? Lessons from the Longest Study on Happiness," TEDxBeaconStreet, November 2015, https://www.ted.com/talks/robert_waldinger _what_makes_a_good_life_lessons_from_the_longest_study_on _happiness.

4   **"three for society":** Henry David Thoreau, *Walden or, Life in the Woods* (Walden Pond, MA: Internet Bookmobile, 2004; originally published 1854).

5   **magazine in 1953:** "Audrey Hepburn: Many-Sided Charmer," *Life* magazine, December 7, 1953.

5   **12,500 miles in 1973:** Chloé, "Hit the Road—Around the World with French Explorer Anne France Dautheville," https://www.chloe. com/experience/us/chloegirls/hit-the-road/.

6   **she was eighty-four:** Gina Kolata, "Dr. Barbara McClintock, 90, Gene Research Pioneer, Dies," *New York Times,* September 4, 1992.

6   *A Return to the Self:* Anthony Storr, *Solitude: A Return to the Self* (New York: Free Press, 1988).

6   **"care to display":** Isaac Asimov, "Isaac Asimov Asks, 'How Do People Get New Ideas?'" *MIT Technology Review,* published with permission of Asimov Holdings, October 20, 2014.

6   **pass on to posterity:** Special cable to the *New York Times,* "$100,000 in Pictures Destroyed by Monet," *New York Times,* May 16, 1908.

6   **into the Arno:** Michael Kimmelman, "Robert Rauschenberg, American Artist, Dies at 82," *New York Times,* May 14, 2008.

7   **"peaceful when desired":** Thuy-vy T. Nguyen, Richard M. Ryan, and Edward L. Deci, "Solitude as an Approach to Affective Self-Regulation," *Personality and Social Psychology Bulletin* 44, no. 1 (October 2017): 92–106. Also: University of Rochester NewsCenter, Rochester.edu.

7   a **"moral inventory":** Alan Westin, *Privacy and Freedom* (New York: IG Publishing, Association of the Bar of the City of New York, 1967).

7   *Research in Personality:* Jerry M. Burger, "Individual Differences in Preference for Solitude," *Journal of Research in Personality* 29, no. 1 (March 1995): 85–108.

7   **"get the alone time":** Bill Clinton, *My Life* (New York: Vintage Books, 2005).

8   **powerful or outsiders:** John D. Barbour, "A View from Religious Studies: Solitude and Spirituality," in *The Handbook of Solitude: Psychological Perspectives on Social Isolation, Social Withdrawal, and Being Alone,* eds. Robert J. Coplan and Julie C. Bowker (West Sussex, UK: John Wiley & Sons, 2014).

8   **(often wrong) distinction:** Burger, "Individual Differences."

8   **selfish and unselfish:** Abraham H. Maslow, *Toward a Psychology of Being* (Jersey City, NJ: Start Publishing, 2012).

8   **solitude can offer:** Burger, "Individual Differences."

8   **detachment, and meditativeness:** Maslow, *Toward a Psychology of Being.*

9   **whether or not it's voluntary:** Nguyen, Ryan, and Deci, "Solitude as an Approach to Affective Self-Regulation."

9   **play a role:** Kenneth H. Rubin, "Foreword: On Solitude, Withdrawal, and Social Isolation," in *The Handbook of Solitude: Psychological Perspectives on Social Isolation, Social Withdrawal, and Being Alone,* eds. Robert J. Coplan and Julie C. Bowker (West Sussex, UK: John Wiley & Sons, 2014).

9   **solitude and excessive loneliness:** James R. Averill and Louise Sundararajan, "Experiences of Solitude: Issues of Assessment, Theory, and Culture," in *The Handbook of Solitude: Psychological Perspectives on Social Isolation, Social Withdrawal, and Being Alone,* eds. Robert J. Coplan and Julie C. Bowker (West Sussex, UK: John Wiley & Sons, 2014).

9   **"trip in Wales":** Charles Darwin, "This Is the Question Marry Not Marry," in *The Complete Work of Charles Darwin Online,* ed. John van Wyhe, 2002, http://darwin-online.org.uk/.

9–10   **"good deal of solitude":** Charles Darwin, "Letter no. 489," Darwin Correspondence Project, accessed on March 3, 2018, http://www.darwinproject.ac.uk/DCP-LETT-489.xml.

10   **six hours a day:** English Heritage, "Description of Down House," http://www.english-heritage.org.uk/visit/places/home-of-charles-darwin-down-house/history/description/.

10   **solve a problem:** Sir Hedley Atkins, *Down: The Home of the Darwins; The Story of a House and the People Who Lived There* (London: Phillimore for the Royal College of Surgeons of England, 1976).

10   **here and now:** Charles Baudelaire, *The Painter of Modern Life and Other Essays,* ed. and trans. Jonathan Mayne (London: Phaidon Press, 1964).

11 **"this being-with-everything":** Rainer Maria Rilke, *Letters of Rainer Maria Rilke, 1892–1910*, trans. Jane Bannard Greene and M.D. Herter Norton (New York: W.W. Norton, 1945).

12 **"to live it":** John Russell, *Paris* (New York: Harry N. Abrams, Inc., Publishers, 1983).

13 **limiting or flat-out unhealthy:** Storr, *Solitude.*

14 **"heart of the multitude":** Baudelaire, *Painter of Modern Life.*

14 **"charmed *flâneur*" in *Italian Hours*:** Henry James, *Italian Hours* (Boston and New York: Houghton Mifflin, 1909).

15 **living in Paris:** Julia Child with Alex Prud'homme, *My Life in France* (New York: Alfred A. Knopf, 2006).

### Café et Pluie ~ Coffee and Rain

21 **"soul is lost":** Eleanor Clark, *The Oysters of Locmariaquer* (New York: Harper Perennial, 2006).

23 **street of writers:** Marquis de Rochegude, *Promenades dans toutes les rues de Paris: 5e Arrondissement* (Internet Archive, Paris: Hachette, 1910), https://archive.org/stream/promenadesdansto05rochuoft#page/n5/mode/2up.

23 **apartment there in the 1700s:** Denis Diderot, *Oeuvres de Diderot*, vol. 1 (Paris: Paulin, 1843).

24 **late-fifteenth century:** Michel Poisson, *Paris Buildings and Monuments: An Illustrated Guide with Over 850 Drawings and Neighborhood Maps* (New York: Harry N. Abrams, Inc., Publishers, 1999).

24 **what is now Turkey:** Anastasia Loukaitou-Sideris and Renia Ehrenfeucht, *Sidewalks: Conflict and Negotiation over Public Space* (Cambridge, MA: MIT Press, 2009).

25 **marshes of Guérande:** Poilâne Bakery, http://laboiteny.com/poilane-bakery.

25 **(Poilâne's bread sculptures):** Meg Bortin, "Apollonia Poilâne Builds on Her Family's Legacy," *New York Times*, June 18, 2008.

26 **rue de Buci:** Les Deux Magots, http://www.lesdeuxmagots.fr/en/history-restaurant-paris.html.

26 **"bread with another":** Oxford University Press, "Companion," https://en.oxforddictionaries.com/definition/companion.

26 **that "emphasizes togetherness":** UNESCO Intangible Cultural Heritage of Humanity List, "Gastronomic Meal of the French," https://ich.unesco.org/en/RL/gastronomic-meal-of-the-french-00437.

28 **"delights of the moment":** Fred B. Bryant and Joseph Veroff, *Savoring: A New Model of Positive Experience* (Mahwah, NJ: Lawrence Erlbaum Associates, 2007).

28 **"baking the batch":** Poilane, "Discover Our Universe," https://www.poilane.com/en_US/page/about.

28 **tips of his fingers:** "PARIS Lionel Poilane THE BAKER," CBS Sunday Morning, video, 3:59, June 7, 2010, YouTube, https://www.youtu.be com/WYOOyNZ5axs.

29 **platter of sole meunière:** Child, *My Life in France.*

29 **bite or sip:** Clark, *Oysters of Locmariaquer.*

29 **"suddenly from the oven":** Jean-Paul Aron, *The Art of Eating in France: Manners and Menus in the Nineteenth Century,* trans. Nina Rootes (New York: Harper & Row, 1975).

30 **"guilt and shame":** Sonja Lyubomirsky, *The How of Happiness: A Scientific Approach to Getting the Life You Want* (New York: Penguin Press, 2008).

30 **psychologist Daniel T. Gilbert:** Matthew A. Killingsworth and Daniel T. Gilbert, "A Wandering Mind Is an Unhappy Mind," *Science* 330, no. 6006 (November 2010): 932.

30 **you are in the present:** Steve Bradt, "Wandering Mind Not a Happy Mind," *Harvard Gazette,* November 11, 2010.

31 **a TEDxCambridge conference:** Matt Killingsworth, "Want to Be Happier? Stay in the Moment," TEDxCambridge, November 2011, https://www.ted.com/talks/matt_killingsworth_want_to_be_happier_stay_in_the_moment.

34 **wife in 1902:** Rilke, *Letters.*

35 **pajamas, drinking Champagne:** Luke Barr, *Provence, 1970: M.F.K. Fisher, Julia Child, James Beard, and the Reinvention of American Taste* (New York: Clarkson Potter, 2013).

35 **his hotel room:** James Beard, *The Armchair James Beard* (New York: Open Road Integrated Media, 2015).

La Vie est Trop Courte Pour Boire du Mauvais Vin ~ Life Is Too Short to Drink Bad Wine

37 **"make it yourself":** Diana Vreeland, *Diana Vreeland: The Eye Has to Travel,* directed by Lisa Immordino Vreeland, Bent-Jorgen Perlmutt, and Frédéric Tcheng, 2011.

38 **"sky," he wrote:** Thich Nhat Hanh, *Peace Is Every Step: The Path of Mindfulness in Everyday Life* (New York: Bantam Books, 1991).

39    **market research company:** The NPD Group/National Eating
      Trends, "Consumers Are Alone Over Half of Eating Occasions as a
      Result of Changing Lifestyles and More Single-Person Households,
      Reports NPD," August 6, 2014, https://www.npd.com/wps/portal
      /npd/us/news/press-releases/consumers-are-alone-over
      -half-of-eating-occasions-as-a-result-of-changing-lifestyles-and
      -more-single-person-households-reports-npd/.

39    **"it is almost fashionable":** Stephen Dutton, "South Korea Sets the
      Standard for Global Solo Dining Trends," *Euromonitor International*,
      August 12, 2016.

39    **"snackification of meals":** "Evolving Trend in Eating Occassions:
      'All by Myself,'" Hartman Group, April 19, 2016.

40    **Economic Cooperation and Development:** Sophie Hardach,
      "Sleeping and Eating—the French Do It Best," *Reuters*, May 4, 2009.

40    **"for the theatre":** Alice B. Toklas, *The Alice B. Toklas Cook Book* (New
      York: Harper Perennial, 2010).

40    **not at mealtime:** Nathaniel Hawthorne, "Concord, May 29th, 1844,"
      *Love Letters of Nathaniel Hawthorne, Volume 2 of 2* (Project Gutenberg,
      2012; originally published 1907).

40    **"Refuses to Dine Alone":** Barrett McGurn, "Pope John's First
      Year—II: He Shatters Tradition, Refuses to Dine Alone," *Daily Boston
      Globe*, October 20, 1959, 25.

41    **not a "with":** Erving Goffman, *Relations in Public: Microstudies of the
      Public Order* (New Brunswick, NJ: Transactions Publishers, 2010).

41    *Personality and Social Psychology:* Thomas D. Gilovich, Victoria
      Husted Medvec, and Kenneth Savitsky, "The Spotlight Effect in Social
      Judgment: An Egocentric Bias in Estimates of the Salience of One's
      Own Actions and Appearance," *Journal of Personality and Social Psychol-
      ogy* 78, no. 2 (2000): 211–22.

42    **search of answers:** Bella DePaulo, "Single in a Society Preoccupied
      with Couples," in *The Handbook of Solitude: Psychological Perspectives on
      Social Isolation, Social Withdrawal, and Being Alone*, eds. Robert J.
      Coplan and Julie C. Bowker (West Sussex, UK: John Wiley & Sons,
      2014).

45    **only for galas:** Aron, *Art of Eating in France*.

46    *A Room of One's Own:* Virginia Woolf, *A Room of One's Own* (New
      York and Burlingame: Harcourt, Brace & World, 1929 and 1957).

46  *New York Times:* "Women's Right to Eat Alone: Republican Club Members Vote for It, but Oppose Sunday Opening," *New York Times,* February 12, 1908.

47  **"experience with that situation":** Craig Claiborne, "Dining Alone Can Pose Problem for a Woman," *New York Times,* June 16, 1964.

47  **"enter a restaurant":** Deborah Harkins, "The City Politic: Sex and the City Council," *New York* magazine, April 27, 1970.

47  **partner, Jill Ward:** Voices of Feminism Oral History Project, Sophia Smith Collection, Smith College, Northampton, MA. Dolores Alexander interviewed by Kelly Anderson, March 20, 2004 and October 22, 2005, Southold, NY.

47  **magazine in 1975:** Jim Jerome, "Feminists Hail a Restaurant Where the Piece de Resistance Is an Attitude, Not a Dish," *People Magazine 3,* no. 21 (June 2, 1975).

47  **about its pleasures:** M.F.K. Fisher, *Gourmet,* 1948.

47  **to "Supper Alone":** Marion Cunningham, *Marion Cunningham's Good Eating: The Breakfast Book; The Supper Book* (New York: Wings Books, 1999).

48  **"reading a book":** "Fran Lebowitz: By the Book," *New York Times,* March 21, 2017.

48–49 **restaurant reservations company:** Caroline Potter, "You're Not Alone: OpenTable Study Reveals Rise in Solo Dining, Names Top Restaurants for Solo Diners," *OpenTable,* October 7, 2015.

49  **parts of Asia, too:** AFP Relaxnews, "Table for one: Solo dining trend is rising in Europe," *Inquirer.net,* May 4, 2017.

49  **Euromonitor has found:** Daphne Kasriel-Alexander, "Top 10 Global Consumer Trends for 2017," *Euromonitor International.*

49  **smell of the food:** "Testing Out Ichiran Ramen's 'Flavor Concentration Booths'—NYC Dining Spotlight, Episode 12," ZAGAT, video, 4:37, November 22, 2016, YouTube, https://www.youtube.com/BxdMZ7Co03s.

49  **tickled by the concept:** Andy Warhol, *The Philosophy of Andy Warhol: From A to B and Back Again* (New York: Harcourt, 1977).

49  **conducive to savoring:** Dutton, "South Korea Sets the Standard."

50  **"is not come":** Frank H Stauffer in the *Epoch,* "Stories About Musicians: Haydn Ate a Dinner for Five—Paesiello's Best Music Was Written in Bed," *Boston Daily Globe,* October 5, 1889.

50  **"companions at the table":** A.J. Liebling, *Between Meals: An Appetite for Paris* (New York: North Point Press, 1986).

# Notes

## A Picnic for One in the Luxembourg Gardens

51  **"place to settle":** Beard, *The Armchair James Beard.*

54  **Aron put it:** Aron, *Art of Eating in France.*

55  **her native Florence:** Paris Tourism website, https://en.parisinfo
.com/paris-museum-monument/71393/Jardin-du-Luxembourg.

55  **associated with ourselves:** John T. Jones, Brett W. Pelham, Mauricio
Carvallo, and Matthew C. Mirenberg, "How Do I Love Thee? Let Me
Count the Js: Implicit Egotism and Interpersonal Attraction," *Journal of
Personality and Social Psychology* 87, no. 5 (November 2004): 665–83.

56  **calls "super-encounterers":** Sanda Erdelez, "Information Encountering; A Conceptual Framework for Accidental Information Discovery," ISIC '96 Proceedings of an international conference on
Information seeking in context, Taylor Graham Publishing, 412–21.

56  **played in their discoveries:** Pagan Kennedy, "How to Cultivate the
Art of Serendipity," *New York Times,* January 2, 2016.

56  **be on hand:** "History Timeline: Post-it Notes", About Us, 3M Corpo-
ration, accessed March 7, 2018, https://www.post-it.com/3M/en_US/
post-it/contact-us/about-us/.

56  **the word's etymology:** Robert K. Merton and Elinor Barber, *The
Travels and Adventures of Serendipity* (Princeton, NJ: Princeton University
Press, 2004).

59  **"deep in the stream":** Woolf, *A Room of One's Own.*

## Of Oysters and Chablis

61  **"quite works out":** Molly O'Neill, "Savoring the World According
to Julia," *New York Times,* October 11, 1989.

61  **"splendour and majesty":** Baudelaire, *Painter of Modern Life.*

63  **"sort of spiritual revolution":** Craig Claiborne, "A Young American's
Palate Gets an Education at Troisgros," *New York Times,* February 12, 1975.

67  **"glass of wine":** "Les Éditeurs," *TimeOut Paris,* August 16, 2013,
https://www.timeout.com/paris/en/restaurants/les-editeurs.

68  **on rue Montorgueil:** Stohrer website, http://stohrer.fr/.

70  **across from a frog:** Casey Baseel, "Sanrio's Kero Kero Keroppi Hops Into
Restaurant Biz with Character Cafe in Japan!" *SoraNews24,* April 25, 2017.

71  **while at La Closerie:** "Hemingway's Paris," *New York Times,* 2006,
http://www.nytimes.com/fodors/top/features/travel/destinations
/europe/france/paris/fdrs_feat_117_11.html.

72  **"enjoy an oyster":** Clark, *Oysters of Locmariaquer.*

Musée de la Vie Romantique

75 **"at our disposal ... ":** Marcel Proust, *Remembrance of Things Past* (New York: Random House, 1949), https://archive.org/details/ost-english -remembranceofthi029925mbp.

76 **Duke Ellington played:** Paris Tourism website, "Paris: the plaque in memory of Gainsbourg unveiled by Jane and Charlotte," Le Parisien, March 10, 2016. Michael Dregni, *Django: The Life and Music of a Gypsy Legend* (New York: Oxford University Press, 2004).

76 **wondered in his journal:** Hubert Wellington, *The Journal of Eugene Delacroix* (London: Phaidon Press, 1995).

77 **toured the museum alone:** Martin Tröndle, Stephanie Wintzerith, Roland Wäspe, and Wolfgang Tschacher, "A Museum for the Twenty-first Century: The Influence of 'Sociality' on Art Reception in Museum Space," *Museum Management and Curatorship*, February 2012.

78 **just in different ways:** Jan Packer and Roy Ballantyne, "Solitary vs. Shared Learning: Exploring the Social Dimension of Museum Learning," *Curator: The Museum Journal* 48, no 2 (2005).

79 **Drake or Debussy:** Stephanie Rosenbloom, "The Art of Slowing Down in a Museum," *New York Times*, October 9, 2014.

81 *Environment and Behavior:* Stephen Kaplan, Lisa V. Bardwell, and Deborah B. Slakter, "The Museum as a Restorative Environment," *Environment and Behavior* 25, no. 6 (November 1, 1993): 725–42.

81 **"tranquillity and personal freedom":** Stéphane Debenedetti, "Investigating the Role of Companions in the Art Museum Experience," *International Journal of Arts Management* 5, no. 3 (Spring 2003).

82 **didn't have many friends:** Ratner and Hamilton, "Inhibited from Bowling Alone."

83 **"visit a friend":** John Steinbeck, *Travels with Charley: In Search of America* (New York: Penguin Books, 1980).

83 **few of the latter:** Paris Tourism website.

86 **someplace more intimate: Parc Monceau:** Marcel Proust, *Swann's Way: Remembrance of Things Past*, vol. 1, trans. C.K. Scott Moncrieff (New York: Henry Holt, 1922).

86 **It attracted banking families:** The Parc Monceau website, http:// madparis.fr/en/museums/musee-nissim-de-camondo/the-mansion -and-the-collections/the-parc-monceau.

86   **banks in the Ottoman Empire:** Les Arts Décoratifs website, http://
www.lesartsdecoratifs.fr/en/museums/musee-nissim-de-camondo/.

87   **than in the desk:** Mervyn Rothstein, "A Parisian Trip to the 1700's,"
*New York Times*, January 20, 1991.

88   **"idea of perfect happiness":** Camille Claudel, "Confessions. An Album to Record Opinions, Thoughts, Feelings, Ideas, Peculiarities,
Impressions, Characteristics," May 16, 1888, http://www.musee
-rodin.fr/en/collections/archives/confessions.

88   **"the Plaine Monceau":** Emile Zola, *Nana, The Miller's Daughter, Captain Burle, Death of Olivier Becaille* (Project Gutenberg, 2006; originally
published 1941).

88   **"corners of Paris":** Henry James, *The American*, produced by Pauline
J. Iacono, John Hamm, and David Widger, 1877.

88   **"something good to eat":** Colette, "Claudine in Paris," in *Colette: The
Complete Claudine*, trans. Antonia White (New York: Farrar, Straus and
Giroux, 1976).

88   **Murillo, Parc Monceau:** George Sand and Gustave Flaubert, *The
George Sand-Gustave Flaubert Letters*, trans. A.L. McKenzie (Project
Gutenberg, 2004; originally published 1921).

88   **once put it:** Gustave Caillebotte, Sotheby's catalogue, "Le Parc Monceau, Impressionist and Modern Art Evening Sale," London, February
5, 2013, http://www.sothebys.com/en/auctions/ecatalogue/2013
/impressionist-modern-art-evening-sale-l13002/lot.32.html.

89   **attempt proved fatal:** S.L. Kotar and J.E. Gessler, *Ballooning: A History, 1782–1900* (Jefferson, NC: McFarland, 2011).

89   **skirting Victorian convention:** Alexandra Lapierre and Christel
Mouchard, *Women Travelers: A Century of Trailblazing Adventures, 1850–
1950*, trans. Deke Dusinberre (Paris: Flammarion, 2007).

90   **she was forty:** Marianne North, *Recollections of a Happy Life, Being
the Autobiography of Marianne North* (New York: Macmillan, 1894).

Window-Licking

91   **"stroll is Parisian":** Victor Hugo, *Les Misérables*, trans. Isabel F. Hap-
good (Project Gutenberg, 2008; originally published 1887).

91   **in the 1960s:** "France May Lose Theater-in-Round," *New York Times*,
September 7, 1964.

93   **more passionate name:** Penelope Green, "BOOKS OF STYLE; Good
to the Last Shop," *New York Times*, November 23, 2003.

Notes

93   **as Balzac wrote:** Honoré de Balzac, trans. Katharine Prescott
     Wormeley, *La Comédie Humaine d'Honoré de Balzac*, vol. 12 (Boston:
     Hardy, Pratt & Company, 1900).
94   **told *InStyle* magazine:** Jennifer Merritt, "Lena Dunham on Being a
     Loner: 'When People Cancel on Me, I Feel Like I Found $1,000,'" *In-
     Style*, June 18, 2016.
95   **Harvard Business School, wrote:** Elizabeth Dunn and Michael
     Norton, *Happy Money: The Science of Smarter Spending* (New York: Si-
     mon & Schuster, 2013).
95   **gives life meaning:** Storr, *Solitude*.
95   **have described it:** Richard M. Ryan and Edward L. Deci, "Intrinsic
     and Extrinsic Motivations: Classic Definitions and New Directions,"
     *Contemporary Educational Psychology* 25, no. 1 (2000): 54–67.
96   **sparked by perambulating:** Marily Oppezzo and Daniel L.
     Schwartz, "Give Your Ideas Some Legs: The Positive Effect of Walking
     on Creative Thinking," *Journal of Experimental Psychology: Learning,
     Memory, and Cognition* 40, no. 4 (2014): 1142–52.
96   **Renoir, and Moreau:** Victor Hugo, *The Memoirs of Victor Hugo* (Proj-
     ect Gutenberg, 2009; originally published 1899). Musée d'Orsay web-
     site, musee-orsay.fr/en/collections/works-in-focus/search
     /commentaire_id/paul-leclercq-10682.html. Jean Renoir, *Renoir: My
     Father* (New York: New York Review of Books Classics, 1958). Stephan
     Wolohojian, ed., with Anna Tahinci, "A Private Passion: Nineteenth-
     Century Paintings and Drawings from the Grenville L. Winthrop
     Collection, Harvard University," Metropolitan Museum of Art, New
     York, 2003.
97   **University of California, Riverside:** Lyubomirsky, *The How of Hap-
     piness*.
97   **an ideal shared space:** The Project for Public Spaces website, https://
     www.pps.org/article/grplacefeat.
97   **"to stroll is to live":** Honoré de Balzac, *The Works of Honoré de Balzac*,
     vol. 36 (New York: McKinlay, Stone and MacKenzie, 1915).
99   ***The Human Comedy:*** Encyclopaedia Britannica, "Honoré de Balzac,"
     https://www.britannica.com/biography/Honore-de-Balzac.
99   **all his works:** Honoré de Balzac, *Letters to Madame Hanska, born
     Countess Rzewuska, Afterwards Madame Honoré de Balzac, 1833–1846*,
     trans. Katharine Prescott Wormeley (Boston: Hardy, Pratt & Com-
     pany, 1900).

# Notes

100 **copious amounts of coffee:** Mary Blume and the *International Herald Tribune* (Paris edition), "Saga of a Statue: The Struggles of Rodin's Balzac," *New York Times*, August 15, 1998.

## Üsküdar

105 **"breathless even, for adventure":** Eartha Kitt with Tonya Bolden, *Rejuvenate! (It's Never Too Late)* (New York: Scribner, 2001).

107 **every apartment window:** Hilary Sumner-Boyd and John Freely, *Strolling Through Istanbul: The Classic Guide to the City* (London: Tauris Parke Paperbacks, 2014).

107 **Brooklyn and Üsküdar:** "New York's Brooklyn Signs Sister City Protocol with Istanbul's Üsküdar," *BGNNews*, Istanbul, August 12, 2015.

107 **"bridges of the soul":** Mehmet Çelik, "Brooklyn-Üsküdar: Istanbul and New York's Iconic Districts Join Forces," *Daily Sabah*, August 12, 2015.

108 **early in her career:** Adrian Jack, "Obituary: Eartha Kitt," *Guardian* (U.S. edition), December 28, 2008.

108 ***Strolling Through Istanbul:*** Sumner-Boyd and Freely, *Strolling Through Istanbul*.

109 **attest to its effectiveness:** Elizabeth W. Dunn, Daniel T. Gilbert, and Timothy D. Wilson, "If Money Doesn't Make You Happy Then You Probably Aren't Spending It Right," *Journal of Consumer Psychology* 21, no. 2 (2011): 115–25.

109 **ten-foot tiger shark:** Stephanie Rosenbloom, "What a Great Trip! And I'm Not Even There Yet," *New York Times*, May 7, 2014.

109 **and "rosy retrospection":** Terence R. Mitchell, Leigh Thompson, Erika Peterson, and Randy Cronk, "Temporal Adjustments in the Evaluation of Events: The 'Rosy View,'" *Journal of Experimental Social Psychology* 33, no. 4 (July 1997): 421–48.

111 **"anywhere in the world":** Andrew Finkel, *The Interior Design of Zeynep Fadillioğlu: Bosphorus and Beyond* (Istanbul: MF Turistik Tesisleri, 2010).

## The Hamam

115 **"as much as possible":** Hussein Chalayan, "Hussein Chalayan on Fitting in," The School of Life lecture series, Vimeo, February 2013, https://vimeo.com/60544453.

115 ***The Innocents Abroad:*** Mark Twain (Samuel Clemens), *The Innocents Abroad* (Project Gutenberg, 2006; originally published 1869).

116   **"as best I can":** Edmondo De Amicis, *Constantinople* (Richmond, UK: Alma Classics, 2013).

117   **industry behemoth TripAdvisor:** Jennifer Polland, "Here's Why Istanbul Is the Most Popular Travel Destination in the World," *Business Insider,* April 8, 2014.

118   **"party capital of Europe":** Andrew Finkel, "Istanbul Thrives as the New Party Capital of Europe," *Guardian* (U.S. edition), January 1, 2011.

118   **are curious people:** Robert Biswas-Diener and Todd B. Kashdan, "What Happy People Do Differently," *Psychology Today,* July 2, 2013.

118   **scientific pursuits, or innovation:** Todd B. Kashdan and Paul J. Silvia, "Curiosity and Interest: The Benefits of Thriving on Novelty and Challenge," in *The Oxford Handbook of Positive Psychology,* eds. Shane J. Lopez and C.R. Snyder (New York: Oxford University Press, 2009), 367–75.

119   **need not be major:** Sonja Lyubomirsky, *The Myths of Happiness: What Should Make You Happy, but Doesn't; What Shouldn't Make You Happy, but Does* (New York: Penguin Press, 2013), 226–27.

120   **a Turkish bath:** Antoine Remise, Gizem Unsalan, and Santiago Brusadin, "The Do's and Dont's of Visiting Istanbul in Summer," *TimeOut Istanbul,* August 8, 2015.

122   **"locker rooms of men":** Gloria Steinem, *Outrageous Acts and Everyday Rebellions* (New York: Holt, Rinehart and Winston, 1983).

123   **than new things:** Leaf Van Boven and Thomas Gilovich, "To Do or to Have? That Is the Question," *Journal of Personality and Social Psychology* 85, no. 6 (2003): 1193–1202. Aaron C. Weidman and Elizabeth W. Dunn, "The Unsung Benefits of Material Things," *Social Psychological and Personality Science* 7, no. 4 (2015): 390–99.

124   **"undermined as much":** Van Boven and Gilovich, "To Do or to Have?"

124   **confidence and self-esteem:** "Outward Bound 2016 Fact Sheet," OutwardBound, https://www.outwardbound.org/about-outward-bound/media.

Call to Prayer

125   **"bore an invitation":** Ahmet Hamdi Tanpinar, *A Mind at Peace,* trans. Erdag Goknar (Brooklyn: Archipelago Books, 1949; English translation, 2008).

126   **"return to ourselves":** Hanh, *Peace Is Every Step.*

127   **magazine in 1928:** "The Story of Greta Garbo," as told by her to Ruth Biery, *Photoplay,* 1928.

# Notes

129 **boatman of the Styx:** Théophile Gautier, *Constantinople of To-day*, trans. Robert Howe Gould (London: David Bogue, 1854).

131 **(to behead her):** Edith Hamilton, *Mythology: Timeless Tales of Gods and Heroes* (New York: A Mentor Book from New American Library, 1969).

131 **"than the model":** Umberto Eco, *Travels in Hyperreality*, trans. William Weaver (San Diego: Harcourt Brace, 1986).

## The Rainbow Stairs of Beyoğlu

135 **"here and now":** Orhan Pamuk, *The Innocence of Objects*, trans. Ekin Oklap (New York: Abrams, 2012).

136 **"act of guerrilla beautification":** Sebnem Arsu and Robert Mackcy, "With a Burst of Color, Turkey's Public Walkways Become a Focus of Quiet Protest," *New York Times*, September 3, 2013.

136 **"a thousand eyes see you":** Edmondo De Amicis, *Constantinople* (Richmond, UK: Alma Classics, 2013).

137 **"bellowing of foghorns":** Leonard Koren, *Wabi-Sabi for Artists, Designers, Poets & Philosophers* (Point Reyes, CA: Imperfect Publishing, 1994 and 2008).

137 ***A Mind at Peace:*** Tanpinar, *A Mind at Peace*.

137 **"past its prime":** Orhan Pamuk, trans. Maureen Freely, *Istanbul* (New York: Knopf, 2004 and 2006).

139 **sign that warned:** Orhan Pamuk, *The Innocence of Objects*, trans. Ekin Oklap (New York: Abrams, 2012).

## Before It's Gone

143 **"before / it's gone":** Rumi, *The Essential Rumi: New Expanded Edition*, trans. Coleman Barks (New York: HarperCollins, 2004).

144 **monastery in California:** Pico Iyer, *The Art of Stillness: Adventures in Going Nowhere* (New York: TED Books, Simon & Schuster, 2014).

146 **once put it:** Chalayan, School of Life lecture series.

146 **dozen were wounded:** Ceylan Yeginsu and Tim Arango, "Istanbul Explosion Kills 10 Tourists, and ISIS Is Blamed," *New York Times*, January 12, 2016.

## Arrows and Angels

153 **"stilled and quieted":** Marcus Aurelius, *Meditations* (Project Gutenberg, 2008).

154 **"itself seemed scanty":** Henry James, *Italian Hours* (Project Gutenberg, 2004; originally published 1909).

154 *The Stones of Florence:* Mary McCarthy, *The Stones of Florence* (New York: Open Road Integrated Media, 1963).

154 **its creator, Filippo Brunelleschi:** Ross King, *Brunelleschi's Dome: How a Renaissance Genius Reinvented Architecture* (New York: Bloomsbury, 2000).

156 **found it in the Arno:** Eve Borsook, *The Companion Guide to Florence* (Suffolk, UK: Companion Guides, 1997).

156 **designed by Michelangelo:** Biblioteca Medicea Laurenziana website, https://www.bmlonline.it/en/settore-monumentale.

157 **siege of 1529:** Giorgio Vasari, *Lives of the Artists*, vol. 1, trans. George Bull (New York: Penguin Books, 1965).

158 **biographer, tells us:** Ascanio Condivi, *The Life of Michelangelo*, 2nd ed., trans. Alice Sedgwick Wohl, ed. Hellmut Wohl (University Park, PA: Pennsylvania State University Press, 1999).

159 **did get engaged:** John Keats, *Letters of John Keats to His Family and Friends*, ed. Sidney Colvin (Project Gutenberg, 2011; originally published 1891).

159 **"means most to me":** Amelia Earhart, letter of February 7, 1931, Noank, CT, to GPP: Amelia Earhart Papers (George Palmer Putnam Collection), Purdue University Libraries, e-Archives.

159 **during the siege:** Vasari, *Lives of the Artists*.

162 **the "Stendhal Syndrome":** Clyde Haberman, "Florence's Art Makes Some Go to Pieces," Special to the *New York Times*, May 15, 1989.

163 *Metropolis M magazine:* Maria Barnas, "Confrontations," *Metropolis M*, 2008.

163 **easy to overlook:** "Gary Snyder," biography by the Poetry Foundation, 2009, https://www.poetryfoundation.org/poets/gary-snyder.

164 **"where to go next":** Magda Lipka Falck, *Anywhere Travel Guide: 75 Cards for Discovering the Unexpected, Wherever Your Journey Leads* (San Francisco: Chronicle Books, 2014).

164 **went into a private space:** "Willoughby Sharp Videoviews Vito Acconci (1973)," http://www.ubu.com/film/acconci_sharp.html.

165 **"decided to follow him":** Sophie Calle and Jean Baudrillard, *Suite venitienne/Please follow me.*, trans. Dany Barash and Danny Hatfield (Seattle: Bay Press, 1988).

Notes

166 **"Don't Be Afraid to Travel Alone":** Ruth Orkin, *American Girl in Italy*, Metropolitan Museum of Art, https://www.metmuseum.org/art/collection/search/271216.

Alone with Venus

167 **"seem to vanish . . . ":** Percy Bysshe Shelley, *Essays, Letters from Abroad, Translations and Fragments*, vol. 2, ed. Mary Shelley (London: Edward Moxon, 1840).

168 **come to his aid:** Vasari, *Lives of the Artists*.

168 **"the diligent hunter-with-a-camera":** Susan Sontag, *On Photography* (New York: RosettaBooks, 2005).

169 **since March 2014:** Hemank Lamba, Varun Bharadhwaj, Mayank Vachher et al., *Me, Myself and My Killfie: Characterizing and Preventing Selfie Deaths* (Ithaca, NY: Cornell University Library, 2016).

170 **in Hartford, Connecticut:** *Catalogue: Patti Smith Camera Solo* (New Haven, CT: Wadsworth Atheneum Museum of Art in association with Yale University Press, 2011).

171 **"where you are":** Fran Lebowitz, *Documentary: "Public Speaking,"* directed by Martin Scorsese, HBO, 2010.

171 **times a day:** Michelle Klein (Facebook's head of marketing for North America), Lecture at the TimesCenter during Social Media Week in New York, February 24, 2016.

172 **education minister, stated:** Hugh Schofield, "The Plan to Ban Work Emails Out of Hours," BBC News, Paris, May 11, 2016.

172 **Apollo and Artemis:** Hamilton, *Mythology*.

The Secret Corridor

177 **"that over yourself":** Leonardo da Vinci, *The Notebooks of Leonardo da Vinci, Complete*, trans. Jean Paul Richter (Project Gutenberg, 2004; originally published 1888).

177 **(did not survive):** Niccolo Machiavelli, *History of Florence and of the Affairs of Italy from the Earliest Times to the Death of Lorenzo the Magnificent* (Project Gutenberg, 2006; originally published 1901).

179 **Francia a fool:** Vasari, *Lives of the Artists*.

179 **"to be restored":** Paula Deitz, "After the Florence Flood: Saving Vasari's 'Last Supper,'" *New York Times*, November 3, 2016.

180 **"day you die":** Lyubomirsky, *The How of Happiness*.

180    **Csikszentmihalyi called "flow":** Martin E. P. Seligman, *Flourish: A Visionary New Understanding of Happiness and Well-Being* (New York: Free Press, 2011). Csikszentmihalyi, *Flow*.

180    **Flow involves that:** Ibid.

181    **"always would be":** Jan Swafford, *Beethoven: Anguish and Triumph* (Boston: Houghton Mifflin Harcourt, 2014).

183    **"would you do?":** Travel Leaders Group, "Survey: 'Travel Etiquette: Americans Answer "What Would You Do?,"'" 2017.

191    **"sabbath of stillness":** Mary McCarthy, *The Stones of Florence* (New York: Open Road Integrated Media, 1963).

The City

197    **"I belong: alone":** Chrissie Hynde, The Pretenders, "Alone," 2016.

200    **skipping town whenever possible:** "The Most Visited Cities in the US," WorldAtlas, accessed March 8, 2017, https://www.world atlas .com/articles/the-most-visited-cities-in-the-us.html.

201    **play called *Sex*:** "Mae West Jailed with Two Producers," *New York Times*, April 20, 1927.

203    **described creative living:** Storr, *Solitude*.

204    **a clipper ship:** Jan Morris, *Manhattan '45* (Boston and London: Johns Hopkins University Press, 1986).

204    **"when you're alone":** Chuck Smith and Sono Kuwayama, interview with Agnes Martin at her studio in Taos, New Mexico, November 1997, https://vimeo.com/ondemand/agnesmartin.

205    **arriving from far-flung places:** New York City Department of Parks and Recreation, "Coenties Slip," https://www.nycgovparks.org /parks/coenties-slip.

207    **"one another as well":** Holland Carter, "Where City History Was Made, a 50's Group Made Art History," *New York Times*, January 5, 1993.

207    **skylights of his studio:** Whitney Museum of American Art, Downtown Branch, *Nine Artists/Coenties Slip*, January 10–February 14, 1974, https://archive.org/details/nineartistscoent18whit.

209    **down to the river:** George Washington, "Rules of Civility & Decent Behaviour in Company and Conversation," University of Virginia, the Washington Papers, http://gwpapers.virginia.edu/about/.

# Notes

## Sanctuaries and Strangers

211 **"on a / Saturday":** Charles Bukowski, "My Secret Life, " in *Sifting Through the Madness for the Word, the Line, the Way: New Poems* (New York: HarperCollins, 2008).

212 **what I do:** Merriam-Webster, "Planet," https://www.merriam-webster.com/dictionary/planet.

213 **SoraNews24 translated it:** Lewis Mumford, *The City in History: Its Origins, Its Transformations, and Its Prospects* (San Diego: Harcourt 1989).

213 **nests to check in:** Winifred Gallagher, *House Think: A Room-by-Room Look at How We Live* (New York: HarperCollins, 2006).

213 **symptoms like headaches:** Judith Heerwagen, "Smart Space: Thinking Outside the Cube," 2004, https://www.creativityatwork.com/2004/09/10/does-your-office-feel-like-a-zoo/.

213 **his "sky parlor":** "Nathaniel Hawthorne," National Park Service, Minute Man National Historic Park, May 24, 2016, https://www.nps.gov/mima/learn/historyculture/thewaysidenathanielhawthorne.htm.

213 **"water and tree room":** Aeronwy Thomas, *My Father's Places: A Memoir by Dylan Thomas's Daughter* (New York: Skyhorse Publishing, 2009).

214 **"opportunities for solitude":** Wilderness Act, Public Law 88-577 (16 U.S.C. 1131–1136), 88th Congress, 2nd Session, September 3, 1964.

214 **who seem like extroverts:** "The Rest Test: A Hubbub Collaboration with BBC Radio 4," 2015, http://hubbubresearch.org.

214 *Lower Back Tattoo:* Amy Schumer, *The Girl with the Lower Back Tattoo* (New York: Gallery Books, 2016).

215 **Lenny Bruce checked in:** C.J. Hughes, "Hopes for a Street Resistant to Rebirth," *New York Times*, October 1, 2013. James Sullivan, "Lenny Bruce Legacy Reexamined," *Rolling Stone*, March 10, 2012.

217 **took their order:** Gillian M. Sandstrom and Elizabeth W. Dunn, "Is Efficiency Overrated? Minimal Social Interactions Lead to Belonging and Positive Affect," *Social Psychological and Personality Science* 5, no. 4 (May 2014): 437–42.

217 **talk to strangers:** Nicholas Epley and Juliana Schroeder, "Mistakenly Seeking Solitude," *Journal of Experimental Psychology: General* 143, no. 5 (2014): 1980–99.

217 **"way of achieving privacy":** Westin, *Privacy and Freedom*.

218 **make us happy are wrong:** Epley and Schroeder, "Mistakenly Seeking Solitude."

218 **perspectives and connections:** Kio Stark, "Why You Should Talk to Strangers," TED2016, February 2016, https://www.ted.com/talks/kio_stark_why_you_should_talk_to_strangers.

218 **attachment to our communities:** The Project for Public Spaces, https://www.pps.org/article/grplacefeat/.

219 **essay "The Stranger":** Georg Simmel, "The Stranger," in *The Sociology of Georg Simmel*, trans. Kurt Wolff (New York: Free Press, 1950).

221 **"you kidding me":** Jen Kirkman, "Just Keep Livin'?," Netflix, 2017.

221 **traveling without men:** Kate Schneider, "Murdered Backpackers Maria Coni and Marina Menegazzo Facebook Post Goes Viral," news.com.au, March 14, 2016.

221 **the victims know:** Stephen J. Dubner, "The Cost of Fearing Strangers," Freakonomics.com, January 6, 2009.

Ode to the West Village

223 **"have to take alone":** Shel Silverstein, "This Bridge," in *A Light in the Attic* (New York: Harper & Row, 1981).

225 **despite the weather:** Alexander Legrain, Naveen Eluru, and Ahmed M. El-Geneidy, "Am Stressed, Must Travel: The Relationship Between Mode Choice and Commuting Stress," *Transportation Research Part F: Traffic Psychology and Behaviour* 34 (October 2015): 141–51.

225 **"What have you not seen?":** Rumi, *Essential Rumi*.

226 **journal entries and letters:** Ting Zhang, Tami Kim, Alison Wood Brooks, Francesca Gino, and Michael I. Norton, "A 'Present' for the Future: The Unexpected Value of Rediscovery," *Psychological Science* 25, no. 10 (October 2014): 1851–60.

227 **Association for Psychological Science:** "Rediscovering Our Mundane Moments Brings Us Unexpected Pleasure," Association for Psychological Science, news release, September 2, 2014.

228 **Arno, near Florence:** Percy Bysshe Shelley, "Florence: Ode to the West-Wind," in *Poems of Places: An Anthology in 31 Volumes. Italy: Vols. XI–XIII. 1876–79*, ed. Henry Wadsworth Longfellow (Boston: James R. Osgood, 1876–79). Bartleby. com, 2011.

# Notes

229   **with whom to break it:** U.S. Census Bureau, data file from Geography Division based on the TIGER/Geographic Identification Code Scheme (TIGER/GICS) computer file. Land area in square miles 2010: 22.83, https://www.census.gov/quickfacts/fact/table/newyorkcoun tymanhattanboroughnewyork/LND110210#viewtop.

## Tips and Tools for Going It Alone

236   **among solo travelers:** Visa Global Travel Intentions Study 2015, prepared by Millward Brown.